The Literate
Kindergarten

The *Literate* Kindergarten

Where Wonder and Discovery Thrive

Susan L. Kempton

Foreword by Susan Zimmermann

HEINEMANN
Portsmouth, NH

Heinemann

361 Hanover Street
Portsmouth, NH 03801–3912
www.heinemann.com

Offices and agents throughout the world

Library of Congress Cataloging-in-Publication Data
Kempton, Susan L.
   The literate kindergarten : where wonder and discovery thrive / Susan L. Kempton ; foreword by Susan Zimmermann.
        p. cm.
   Includes bibliographical references and index.
   ISBN-10: 0-325-00833-7
   ISBN-13: 978-0-325-00833-2
   1. Kindergarten—Activity programs. 2. Kindergarten—Curricula. 3. Children—Books and reading.   I. Title.

LB1180.K46 2007
372.19—dc22   2007025645

Editors: Thomas Newkirk *and* Jane Harrigan
Production: Vicki Kasabian
Cover design: Shawn Girsberger
Typesetter: Tom Allen, Pear Graphic Design
Manufacturing: Louise Richardson

Printed in the United States of America on acid-free paper
11 10 09 08   EB   2 3 4 5

To the best teachers,
all my kindergartners

Contents

Foreword

Five years ago, in 2002, I visited Sue Kempton's kindergarten at Harrington Elementary, a school in a tough part of Denver that serves some of the city's poorest children. A half dozen of us stood at the back of her room as her kindergartners filed in. Within minutes, Sue began working her magic. Among the menagerie of live things—a much-beloved bunny, class snake, toads, caterpillars, eggs waiting to hatch—the children sang, danced, wrote the stories of their lives, created imaginary worlds with big blocks, played house, learned numbers by counting the days of the month, then sang and danced some more, with Sue always leading the way. I left that day feeling both uplifted and downcast. I was, quite simply, blown away by what I had experienced. "What if," I wondered, "all children in America started school in this type of rich, engaging environment and if it continued throughout their school years?" No doubt many of the problems facing education in America would be solved. But the warmth, engagement, fun, and rigor of Sue's kindergarten set a standard I feared was rarely met.

In the early 1990s, I had observed Sue at Asbury Elementary, a school in a more affluent part of Denver, where she then worked. I asked Sue why she had moved to Harrington, a school with a dedicated staff, but with challenges many schools in the Denver system didn't face. Her response was something along the lines that she loved her children; they really needed her; and, if it could be done at Harrington, it could be done anywhere.

I returned to Sue's classroom many times over the years, each time marveling at her energy and adeptness as well as her ability to turn the simplest everyday tasks—

taking attendance, jumping rope at recess—into meaningful learning opportunities for her charges. There was a seamlessness as the children segued gracefully from the oval, where they sat cross-legged and talked about their lives, shared personal learnings, and listened to and discussed books Sue read, to the writing area, where they pulled out their daybooks and wrote and illustrated stories, to the area where they clustered and learned scientific concepts as they watched their pet snake molt or a caterpillar metamorphose into a butterfly. Interspersed throughout the day were music and movement, laughter and conversation. It looked effortless and joyful.

In fact, Sue's approach to teaching five- and six-year-olds is based on years of study, in-the-trenches experience, and an openness and confidence of mind that allow her to observe and listen to her students intently. Committed to educating the whole child, and to making school fun and rewarding, Sue has adopted an educational philosophy based on three equally important domains: creative, cognitive, and emotional. These domains intersect, knit together, and reinforce one another each day. They provide the anchor for all of the work that goes on in Sue's classroom, the vital legs of a three-legged stool that would collapse if one leg was too short or absent. By weaving a tapestry of creative, cognitive, and emotional work into her classroom, Sue creates a community of learners who care about one another, who own their learning, and who feel safe to stretch intellectually and imaginatively. And they are in kindergarten.

The day I finished reading *The Literate Kindergarten: Where Wonder and Discovery Thrive*, I said to my husband, "I didn't think she could do it, Paul. It seemed too hard to capture her classroom on paper. But she has."

"What does she do?" he asked.

"She shows over and over again how smart children are—and she's teaching some of the poorest children in Denver. She never talks down to her children. She always honors their thinking and allows them to follow passions and interests. She teaches them to read, and they love it. She uses play as a way to teach them about math and science. She has them write the stories of their lives. They love being in school and they learn constantly. Mainly, she shows other teachers how they can do this, too. She gives example after example. What she has to share is so, so important."

And it is. In this era when too often test scores are viewed as the full measure of a student's learning and schools are constantly under the gun to get scores up, Sue's is a voice of reason and effectiveness. Thoughtfully, carefully, lovingly, Sue honors children's native intelligence and curiosity and shows that academic rigor and play go hand in hand. She makes it clear that kindergartners are not miniature adults but children who are learning machines fully equipped with a sense of wonder and awe at the world around them. *The Literate Kindergarten* shows in no uncertain terms that true learning occurs, not while sitting quietly confined to a desk chair, but through exploration and play. This very important book reaffirms the beauty and uniqueness of children's developing minds and the power that is unleashed when their imaginations are nurtured.

—SUSAN ZIMMERMANN
coauthor of 7 *Keys to Comprehension* and *Mosaic of Thought*

Acknowledgments

When I think of how I came to be the teacher I am today, I immediately go back to my earliest preschool experience at Huntington Cooperative Nursery School, driving life-size tractors around a curvy cement pathway that stretched for miles (in my mind), tapping maple trees, painting, hammering at workbenches . . .

Beverley Howe, with help from her husband, Tom, ran this incredible preschool co-op in the mid-1950s, bringing life, joy, and purpose to learning. I have little recollection of my subsequent years in public education, and I vowed to myself that if I chose to go into teaching, I would create a stimulating, fun environment for all children. I thank you both for providing me this grounding foundation in experiential learning.

To my mother, Gloria Lawrence, for helping me see that teaching *is* my passion at a time when I doubted that, and to my dad, William (Bill) Lawrence, for enriching my life with drama and a love of words.

To David Anderson, my cooperating teacher, for setting me on a path of experiential teaching; I'll never forget the mud pathways children cooperatively constructed near the Arizona washes, drawing water to "their" Anazazi farms.

To Ellin Keene and Susan Zimmermann, for bringing your brilliant work into classrooms through your seminal book, *Mosaic of Thought*.

To Rosann Ward, Suzanne Plaut, Lori Conrad, Brooke O'Drobinak, Judy Hendricks, and all those who have contributed to the Public Education and Business Coalition (PEBC), an organization dedicated to providing quality literacy experiences across all content areas; I'm proud to represent you. Thank you for planting the seed of continual reflection and articulation of beliefs and values about children and learning.

To all PEBC lab teachers everywhere, especially Barb Smith, Carrie Symons, Patrick Allen, Susan McIver, Jo Franklin, Troy Rushmore, Leslie Leyden, Cris Tovani, Cheryl Zimmerman, Bruce Morgan, Karen Anderson Berg, Leslie Blauman, Carol Quinby, Rachel Rosenburg, Veronica Moreno—it's a privilege to sit at the same table as you.

To all PEBC staff developers for the insightful facilitation you provide observing teachers; special appreciations to Chryse Hutchins, Kathy Haller, Lori Conrad, Missy Mathews, Kristin Venable, Jennifer Shouse, Sam Bennett, Leanna Harris, Joy Hood, Linda Erickson, Kim Schmidt, Leanne Cantalupo, Ligia Gibson, Ilana Spiegel, and Annie Patterson for your wisdom and connecting learning for visitors.

To Kathy Haller, a personal mentor to me, who I met as a lab participant and later welcomed into my classroom as a staff developer—thank you for setting the tone and expectation of a rigorous, joyful kindergarten and for passing the PEBC class torch to me; I'm forever gratefuf for seeing what's possible.

To my colleagues and friends at Harrington: I'm honored to work beside such a dedicated and supportive staff, committed to improving the education of children who are at risk. Thank you for bringing balance, humor, and love to our strenuous jobs.

To my teammates Emily Rowland, Norma Zoetewey, Christina Jensen, and former teammate Jessica Buckley, for embracing the work I've shared, and taking on kindergarten with full force. Knowing all of you were my support system as I completed this book meant the world to me.

To my principal and assistant principal, Sally Edwards and Cindy Miller, for the relentless support you provide on a daily basis to me and the entire staff. Thank you for trusting and providing me the space to continue the work I do with children.

To Marjory Ulm, for believing in me when I first came to Harrington and supporting me to preserve what I know is best for kids. Thank you for listening, sharing ideas, and helping me see the additional tools to give children. Your insightfulness and years of expertise with this population are astounding.

To Leigh Peake, Vicki Kasabian, and the entire staff at Heinemann, who expertly guided this manuscript through the production process—and to Shawn Girsberger for her awesome cover design.

To Debbie Miller, for inspiring me to write this book; thank you for being a powerful mentor and leading the way!

To Steph Harvey, I'm forever grateful you landed Lois in front of me that hot, sweaty spring day on the Harrington playground. Thank you for years of support, enthusiasm, and encouragement you gave me in my early years of teaching—continually validating my thinking and work during precious years as a developing teacher.

To my treasured paraprofessionals, Natalie Lovato (now a wonderful teacher), and Lisa Aguado (soon to be another great educator), for their remarkable daily support given to me and the children. Thank you both for being my right arm and continually listening to my guidance to improve instruction.

To Paresh Rana, for the beautiful photos you captured.

To Jill Moore and Kathy Graziano: thank you for dedicating your valuable time to read weekly with the children and buying live food for our animal friends—I miss you both!

To Pat Lusche, for the awesome work you have given to the field of reading—and for sharing this with me.

To Lori Conrad, for being my reader and providing me the eyes of a new teacher. Thank you for continually nudging me to clarify and reorganize my thinking, helping me create what I've always dreamed would be helpful for teachers.

To Susan Zimmermann, for the touching, perceptive acknowledgments of my teaching you gave during each and every visit to Harrington; they were nuggets of gold that left me inspired! Thank you for writing such a beautiful foreword; you truly understand the work I do with children.

To Lois Bridges, my first editor and friend: thank you for creating the context for me to write; you gave me what I give my children. Your gentle direction, "Just a few words and away we'll go!," gave me all the confidence to trudge onward.

To Tom Newkirk and Jane Harrigan, my second set of editors, for pushing me to clarify my thinking, simplify ideas, eliminate fluff and reorganize. Jane—I couldn't resist the "list"—thank you for working so closely with me to bring my voice to the front and make this "heady stuff" real. Your expertise is a true gift, and your friendship a blessing! I had the best of both worlds being under the tutelage of you both, and Lois.

To my darling daughter, Lilli, for your patience and perseverance, knowing someday Mommy would be finished writing. You kept me going by reading Junie B. books and writing continually by my side, borrowing markers, stapler, tape, and being my kitty cat.

To my dear husband, Brian, a man of extraordinary talents: thank you for astutely listening to my teaching the past fifteen years; for reading, rereading, and rereading every word of this manuscript; for your artistic photographic and computer talents—I'd be lost without your support; and for your patience and your unconditional love throughout this process, for shopping, cooking, doing laundry, and for the tender care of our precious Lil. Most of all, I thank you for passionately believing in the work I do with children and standing by my side so I could accomplish my lifelong dream.

The Literate Kindergarten

Introduction

A mind stretched by a new idea can never go back to its original dimension.
—Oliver Wendell Holmes

Twenty-five years ago, when I began teaching kindergarten, work and play maintained a peaceful balance in the classroom. By the end of the school year, five- and six-year-olds were expected to be able to write their names and to identify letters and numbers, shapes and colors. But teachers placed at least as much emphasis on creating and then nurturing stimulating play environments. Playhouses, blocks, easels, and workbenches were as essential to the classroom as teaching ABCs and 123s.

Today the emphasis has shifted. Kindergartens now look and feel like watered-down first-grade classrooms. A passerby is much less likely to hear robust singing bellowing into the corridors, hammers banging away at the workbench, loud laughter, or questioning voices. Children have less freedom to move around, exploring science tables or assembling giant towers of blocks, choosing their own ways to interact with one another and materials.

Visitors to today's kindergartens often miss the days when children would set out on imaginary trips downtown, adorned with fluffy fuchsia boas, strands of pearls, wide-brimmed hats, and white gloves. They miss seeing children intently working at the easel, exploring brilliant colors, creating masterpieces as if they had all the time in the world. If today's kindergarten had a soundtrack, it might feature Judy Collins singing, "Where have all the playhouses gone? Long time passing. Where have all the big blocks gone? Long time ago."

Today's kindergarten rooms feel different. It's not that play areas have disappeared, but fewer teachers take time to maintain or use them well. The rigorous demands placed on kindergartners have shifted teachers' focus to academics. As a result, we are impoverishing precious areas of social, emotional, and creative life in the developing child. And in so doing, we disrespect the innocence of this age. With all the pressure to accomplish ever higher academic objectives, it's no wonder that some teachers have lost sight of the big picture. Even with all my teaching experience, I find it harder each year to keep the balance between play and cognitive work. But we have to continue trying, or joy and lightness—the essence of kindergarten—will fade away.

Every kindergarten teacher faces the big question: How do we preserve children's innocence while holding them accountable for increasing academic demands? As I've watched attitudes change over the years, I've developed my own answers. I believe that we kindergarten teachers need a clear vision of academic goals, a plan for turning that vision into reality, and a method for balancing the strenuous academic day with song, movement, talk, and stimulating play.

If ever there was a time when play and creativity were essential, it is now. Children need a creative way to release their energy so they can accommodate more information. The whole point of kindergarten, after all, is to capitalize on a child's natural inclination to talk, move, and sing—to use play to bring forth new learning. When I say *play*, I'm not talking just about recreation and fun. In a broader sense, play encompasses all sorts of sensory-based environments where children can explore and interact, both with others and with a variety of materials. In these environments, children are most themselves. Play is their natural language and thus the best way to see their learning process. As they play—as they touch, talk, observe, listen, explore—children naturally question, discover, and feel, operating in what I refer to as the three domains.

Educators create contexts for children to learn in. The essential foundation for good teaching has three parts: cognitive contexts, where children explore, ask questions, and critically reason; creative contexts, where children put together new learning; and emotional contexts, where children freely express feelings. I refer to these as the cognitive, creative, and emotional domains. I haven't always used those terms; they developed over years of watching and listening to children, years of reflecting on what I do as a teacher and why.

Some of the *why* is easy: Like all teachers, I remember myself as a learner. I was a quiet child; I had no voice to articulate the things I wondered, discovered, or felt. I didn't participate in my education; I simply absorbed and observed. So each August when my new kindergartners stare at me timidly, I see myself in their silence. I know that the shouts, the questions, the *aha!* moments are in there, waiting to come out. Five-year-olds are intensely alive in the here and now, even if they don't yet have the words to express what they're thinking or feeling. As a teacher, I focus all my energy on drawing out that aliveness and helping it take form in language. My job is not just to help children learn but to show them what learning means and how it happens. My job is to make learning visible.

To understand what I mean by the three domains, keep that word *visible* in mind. How you teach depends on how you see. You choose the contexts through which you see your classroom and the world, and you're in charge; you can change those contexts and thus change the entire experience, not just for your students but for yourself. Reflecting on your teaching means becoming conscious of the lenses through which you view the world. For me, there are three: the cognitive, creative, and emotional domains.

Picture it this way: You're sitting in an optometrist's office, and the three domains are three separate lenses the doctor is flipping down for you to look through. You can look through the lenses individually, or two at a time, or all three at once. With each shift, you see things slightly differently, and each of those kinds of vision works well for its own particular purpose.

As a teacher, you need all three lenses, or domains, to see the whole child and understand his learning process. You need the individual lenses to recognize what's going on in the child's mind at any given moment and to bring that internal process out into the light, where both of you can examine it and work with it.

All this may sound abstract at first, but for me, it's a concrete process with specific steps that focus on language. When you carefully watch and listen to children, you realize that their talk and body language shift as they move from something they're wondering about, to something they're learning, to something they're feeling. In other words, children naturally operate from the three domains: they think, discover, and feel all day long.

In teaching, I use the three domains to help children develop a vocabulary that works with each. For example, I begin the year modeling the language of critical thinking and reasoning: "Why does . . . ? I wonder . . . I discovered . . . This is really cool! I get it!" At first, I'm the only one using this language, but gradually some children join in, becoming models for their classmates. They are developing a learning vocabulary and simultaneously developing their own lenses for looking at the world.

The whole process begins to circle in on itself: As students become familiar with the language, they're more able to express thoughts and feelings, which makes them more aware of what's happening inside them. As they become more aware and expressive, they begin to direct their own learning, and both their classmates and I are more able to help because language is showing us the way. In other words, context empowers learning.

I used this approach for many years with kindergartners from affluent backgrounds, and now I'm using it in a school whose students have had many fewer opportunities.

This book shows how I do it: how one teacher's awareness of the three domains helps learning happen. The roots of learning begin in a social milieu; it's up to teachers to provide stimulating contexts where those roots can become living plants that grow and flower. Weaving together the cognitive, creative, and emotional domains gives depth and breadth to a classroom.

At a time when everyone from principals to state and federal regulators demands more proof of academic achievement, many teachers believe their only recourse is to compromise play in favor of more structured lessons. I invite you to consider another idea: Only through the rich social environments created by play will kindergartners succeed in this new rigor. Only if we follow children's natural inclinations, encourage their creativity and openness, can they develop confidence and a love for learning that will last a lifetime.

Underlying Threads

Lenses for Learning

1

The loftiest edifices need the deepest foundations.
—George Santayana

One day during reading workshop, Kasmira (*Kaz-MEER-ah*) approached me, pointing animatedly to a photograph of a snail in a *Zoobooks* magazine. She didn't say a word, but her body language—eyes wide, mouth open, face pushing close to mine—clearly conveyed, "Look at *this*!"

"Did you discover something?" I asked.

Nodding eagerly, she read, "The snail has a strong . . ." The next words were *muscular foot*, but Kasmira came to an abrupt halt when she encountered *muscular*. I asked her to try again, "getting her mouth ready" for the unknown word by forming the sound *muh*.

The word *muscular* flew out of her mouth! I was surprised that she had decoded such a difficult word, which wasn't part of her known vocabulary. "Does this make sense to you?" I asked.

"No," she responded.

"Sweetheart, do you hear a word that sounds familiar in the word *muscular*?"

Perplexed and shaking her head, she repeated, "No."

I gave her physical clues, flexing and pointing to my arm.

Her eyes lit up. "*Muscle*!"

"Yeah!" I responded enthusiastically. "What does *muscle* mean? If you have muscles, what do they give you?"

"Energy?" she asked tentatively.

"Well, that's good thinking, but not exactly. Think about what they give you, what you can do." Again, I pointed at my arm and flexed.

"Strength!" Kasmira said.

"Yeah, they give you strength, so you can lift things and move things. So, *muscular* means . . ."

"Strong!" Kasmira said.

"Yes, the snail has a foot that's really strong. Let's go back and reread the caption and see if it makes sense now." She reread the sentence, and once again I asked, "Does it make sense to you now, Kasmira?"

I was feeling good about this interaction. I had recognized what Kasmira needed and patiently helped her along, and now I was ready for that great moment when the light would dawn. But it didn't. "No," Kasmira said; she still didn't understand what she'd read. Kasmira was a bright, fluent reader, great at using decoding skills. She'd so eagerly embraced the challenge of figuring out what *muscular* meant. Why couldn't she understand the sentence the word came from?

When you hit a wall like this with a student—the kind of small obstacle that teachers bump into a hundred times a day—it's tempting to surrender to frustration. "Come on!" your inner voice is saying. "What's so hard? The answer is right there!" But of course the answer is obvious only to grown-up you, not to a five-year-old. At moments like these, you have to remember those lenses through which we all see the world, remember that children don't use the same lenses that adults do. At moments like these, you have to remember what you believe in—wonder and self-discovery.

All teachers have a set of principles, self-evident truths that, consciously or not, guide their teaching. These are mine:

- Children are naturally intelligent.
- Children are intrinsically motivated to learn.
- Children are innately curious about the world and how it operates.
- Children put together concepts unique to them.
- Emotions connect us to ourselves.
- Sharing connects us to community.
- Community connects us to the world.

Together, these principles and a collection of best practices form my paradigm for teaching. At the core of my beliefs lie the three domains: cognitive, creative, and emotional. The terms may sound complicated, but their genesis was simple: watching and listening to children during my twenty-five years of teaching kindergarten. What are the students wondering? Discovering? Feeling? I've learned to pay attention to the verbal and nonverbal cues that provide a window into their minds. Then, by carefully selecting the words I use when asking about those internal processes, and by helping the children develop a vocabulary for describing their own thoughts and feelings, I can keep track of where each child is in the learning process at any given moment and find ways to help her move along.

For example, my students know that I will stop and listen to *why* questions and to statements that begin "I discovered . . ." or "I'm really mad or sad about . . ." So they take the time to organize their thoughts or feelings into words they know will elicit a response. They also learn from listening to their friends' questions, discoveries, and feelings and from listening to mine. My students regularly hear me asking questions like "What are you wondering?" (cognitive domain), or, as with Kasmira, "What did you discover?" (creative domain), or "What are you feeling?" (emotional domain). The repetition encourages them to use the same language.

Once you can readily identify the domains and the words associated with them, learning becomes more explicit and deliberate for everyone. At any given moment, both teachers and students can recognize that someone is questioning (cognitive domain), discovering (creative domain), or sharing an emotional experience (emotional domain). As my interaction with Kasmira continued, all three domains came into play.

■ Taking Time to Search for Comprehension

The day before Kasmira shared her discovery, our librarian, Mrs. Kayser, had read the children *Are You a Snail?*—a beautifully written and illustrated nonfiction book by Judy Allen (2000). We had snails in our room, and Mrs. Kayser knew that we were carefully observing, talking, and writing about their behavior.

Aide (*AH-day*) and Kasmira had already noticed the snails crawling slowly up the sides of the tank with their feelers popping out of their heads. Quenon (*Quin-NON*) had noticed the snails making little holes in the apples as they ate them. Marcos wondered why snails stick on things. The students wrote their observations and taped them near the snails' tank for all to appreciate.

Mrs. Kayser left *Are You a Snail?* in our classroom for further reading. So when Kasmira came to me with her question about the *Zoobooks* caption, I said, "Get the snail book Mrs. Kayser read yesterday. It might help you understand the snail's foot." After thinking about Kasmira's confusion, I'd figured out that the problem probably was not the word *muscular*. She could make sense of the word in isolation but still couldn't comprehend its meaning in context. Perplexed, I'd asked myself what was missing. I had realized she needed more support in generating a definition for the word *foot* that was different from the familiar definition.

Miguel, listening intently, raced across the floor and snatched the book, which was standing by the snail's tank. "Here, Kasmira," he said proudly.

"Thanks, sweetheart; what a great helper you are!" It's powerful to see children being drawn into one another's inquiries and using tools to support one another's learning.

"Kasmira, see if you can find the part in the book where it talks about the strong foot and reread that paragraph," I said. "It might help." She eagerly took the book and thirty seconds later came back, identifying the section that mentioned the foot. A huge, beautiful illustration of the snail and its foot spanned both pages.

"Good for you! Boy, that was quick! Reread this part to me." She reread *Are You a Snail?* fluently, describing the appendage that helps the snail glide along the damp ground, leaving a sticky trail behind it: "You have a shell with a beautiful pattern on it. You have no legs and only one foot, but it is a strong foot. The slime on your strong foot helps you slide along. Wherever you go, you leave a silvery, slimy trail."

"Now does it make sense?"

"No," she said with a discouraged sigh.

"Do you see something in the illustration?" I asked. "Look closely." I purposely didn't point to the illustration and say, "There is the foot!" I encouraged her to listen to the language and infer what the words described. Decoding words and understanding their meaning in isolation isn't enough to comprehend text. Kasmira knew *muscular* meant strong, but she needed to place the meaning in the text in order to make sense of the whole.

Returning to class after lunch, I explained to the children that Kasmira had done some awesome reading and thinking about snails today, but she was still confused about what a snail's foot looked like. "Could you guys help her figure this out? She needs your help!" Whenever issues arise that leave a child confused or frustrated, I elicit the help of the community. Kids love the opportunity to support a friend. By opening up the discussion to the class, I send a strong message that we are all teachers and learners.

We reread the descriptive paragraph from the book as I displayed a large illustration of the snail. Quenon's eyes lit up. "I get it!" he shouted. "It's that thing sticking out under the snail!"

"Yes, great job! You're absolutely right. That piece of muscle under the snail's body is called its foot. Does it look like ours, with five toes?"

"No!" the kids chimed in, giggling.

"Isn't it funny that it's still called a foot even though it doesn't look anything like ours? Let's reread this part. What you are looking at is its foot. Does it make sense to you now, Kasmira?"

A proud smile spread across her face. "Yeah!" she said.

"Kasmira, remember when you and Aide were watching the snail crawl slowly up the side of the tank? Well, you were looking at his foot! It took a lot of strength for him to carry himself and his shell up the side of the aquarium."

■ What We Can Learn

Cognitive Domain

The cognitive domain is the space where knowledge, understanding, questioning, critical reasoning, inference, and wonder about the world arise. By listening for and drawing out these questions through language, and sharing them with the community, a teacher empowers children to take charge of their learning.

To help children enter the cognitive domain, I use specific language and kinds of questions:

- What are you wondering about?
- Did you discover something?
- Describe what you see. What do you think is happening?
- Does this make sense?
- What do you know? Tell me more.
- If this is true, and this is true, what can you tell me?

This talk leads to dynamic conversations and rigorous thought. In Kasmira's case, she was operating in the cognitive domain when she pointed to the illustration of the snail. I read her body language and knew she had noticed something in her reading before I even asked, "Did you discover something?"

After encouraging her to reread the text and supporting her in decoding the word *muscular*, I asked a series of questions: "Does this make sense to you? Do you hear a word that sounds familiar in the word *muscular*? What does *muscle* mean? If you have muscles, what do they give you?" The questions prompted her to use other thinking strategies, delving more deeply into the cognitive domain.

Inquiry is the basic tool I use to help children to develop strategies like questioning, inferring, and using critical reasoning. In addition, I continually listen to their language and watch their nonverbal cues so that the silent questions inside their heads can come out and lead to learning. In other words, the process of bringing out what is known or wondered about happens in the cognitive domain. The creation of new knowledge unfolds in the creative domain.

Creative Domain

In the creative domain, both teachers and children build and express new learning. So, for example, after encouraging Kasmira to listen for a familiar word within *muscular*, I helped her move toward the creative domain when I prompted, "Think about what muscles give you, what you can do." After she responded *strength*, I reaffirmed its meaning and continued, "So, *muscular* means . . ." With this support, she was able to define *muscular* for herself; this was new learning. Then, when we expanded the inquiry to the whole class, Quenon generated a new definition for the word *foot*, once again gaining access to the creative domain.

The teacher supports the creative domain by designing situations in which children are responsible for their learning. After a child describes what she observes, or what she is wondering, the teacher uses a series of prompts like "If this is true and that is true, what can you tell me about this?" or, simply, "What did you discover?" The questions allow the thoughts and questions that began in the cognitive domain to unfold naturally in the creative domain.

Children generate new learning long before they can articulate or act on it. Through awareness of the domains, teachers encourage thoughtful talk and provide tools and materials that help students recognize their own thought processes and express them in words or actions.

The creative domain can be self-generated or socially generated. Learning takes form when children speak or write their ideas or use materials—paper, glue, scissors, markers, wood, hammers, drills—to put those ideas into action. By nudging children to articulate their thinking and explore different mediums, teachers help them create new information and artifacts, unique to each individual.

Emotional Domain

The emotional domain is where feelings unfold. As conversation and precise language draw out a child's experiences, emotional vocabulary develops and connects to other children's experiences and to reading. Children are whole beings; they need a safe, nurturing environment where feelings can surface and be processed. To focus solely on nurturing intellect is to neglect a significant motivator.

To help children gain access to the emotional domain, I ask questions such as "How are you feeling? What's going on?" Frequently, a child's first response is to shrug, stay silent, or blurt out accusations against another child. Kindergartners don't have the language to articulate what they are feeling; they need help putting emotions into words. So I share my observations of their body language and use the opportunity to help them develop emotional vocabulary.

For example, one day during choice time, I saw Keishon with his head in his hands, sighing loudly. "Keishon, I notice you're trying to build a really cool fort, like the kids did yesterday, and it keeps collapsing," I said. "Do you want some help?" He gave a slight nod. I flicked the lights to gain the other children's attention. "Guys, listen up. Keishon is feeling really frustrated right now. He wants to build a fort like Francisco and Cesar did yesterday, but he can't make it work. Would someone like to help him?"

If this were the first time I'd used the word *frustrated*, I would have reinforced the new vocabulary at the end of play time, acknowledging the children who had supported Keishon. (That would be a great opportunity to introduce the word *supported* as well.) Connecting vocabulary to a child's experience or to a piece of literature can be done immediately or later, or both.

When Kasmira was wondering about the snail's foot, I didn't focus on developing the rich range of emotional vocabulary that presented itself. At the time, it was more important simply to notice the feelings she was experiencing so that I could find ways to connect them with other students and our classroom materials.

If you look back at Kasmira's story, you can see the emotions that surfaced:

- *Excited*: She noticed that the slimy appendage she'd seen underneath the snail sliding up the side of the aquarium was the same thing she saw in the illustration.
- *Uncertain*: She encountered the unknown word *muscular*.
- *Excited*: She discovered that *muscular* means *strong*.
- *Confused*: She didn't understand the word's meaning in context.
- *Frustrated*: She still wasn't understanding the passage.
- *Hopeful*: The community came together in support.
- *Proud*: She came to understand the meaning, completing her inquiry.

When thoughts, memories, experiences, or information is presented together with an emotional link, children are more likely to retain it. Effective teachers naturally link emotional experience to teaching. When we do this consciously, instruction becomes even more precise and purposeful. I focus on the emotional domain in order to help students do more cognitive work while strengthening the classroom community and building mutual respect. As human beings, we are continually feeling, thinking, and creating.

Understanding our emotions and what to do with them broadens our adaptability and our tolerance. When children express emotions, their capacity to learn expands.

Teachers can encourage learning in the emotional domain by listening to children, dealing with situations as they arise, providing time and space for children to talk, and helping them build emotional vocabulary. Doing so honors and supports that vulnerable space in all of us.

Where to Start

- As you create your lesson plans, work on becoming conscious of the lenses through which you're viewing your class. Do your practices reflect your beliefs and values?

- Listen to students as you teach. What are they wondering about? What have they figured out? How might their emotional experiences connect to other children or to class materials?

Cognitive
- Model your own sense of wonder about the world.
- Provide opportunities for open discussion where everyone can ask questions and clarify ideas. Listen to what students already know and what they're trying to figure out.

Creative
- Listen for opportunities to connect pieces of information for a child or between children.
- Ask questions that stimulate reflection and require connecting ideas and concepts together.
- Look for ways to anchor students' learning using movement and other sensory experiences.

Emotional
- Watch for body language or words that provide cues to a child's emotional state.
- Help children share emotional experiences, then use the sharing to define and develop emotional vocabulary.
- Connect this experience to another child's or to literature. Or for experiences involving multiple children, focus on drawing out the emotions they might all share.

Table 1–1 lists some verbal and physical cues you can look for as a teacher to help expand learning in the three domains.

TABLE 1–1 *Verbal and Physical Cues in the Three Domains*	
Domain	**Cues**
Cognitive	• Curiosity, confusion, or focused interest in a child's facial expression or body language • "Why does . . . ?" • "What does . . . mean?" • "Will . . . happen?" • "What if . . . ?" • "Who is . . . ?" • "When . . . ?"
Creative	• A small or large shift in a child's demeanor, facial expression, or body language • "Look, come here! . . . See what I've made!" • "Cool! . . . Mrs. Kempton, I found that thing you were talking about!" • "I discovered . . ."
Emotional	• A shift in a child's demeanor, facial expression, or entire body language. This could be subtle or a blatant appearance of any emotion. • Sounds associated with emotions—sighs, giggles, moans, grunts, short inhalations of breath • "Mrs. Kempton, . . . she won't . . ." or "He just [scribbled] on my . . ."

2 Setting the Tone

A Glimpse of the Day

The real journey of discovery consists not in seeking new landscape, but in having new eyes.

—Marcel Proust

Teachers who visit my kindergarten classroom in November see a veritable twelve-ring circus of learning. First thing in the morning, children are checking out classroom books for homework and energetically performing various classroom rituals and jobs. Some kids are singing favorite songs, following the words on charts hung on a stand, while others are spread out on the carpet, reading all kinds of books and magazines, alone or in groups. If you hover near one of those groups, you'll hear enthusiastic talk and constant questions.

At a signal from me, everyone scurries about the room, returning books to their proper places; within seconds the students are seated cross-legged on the oval, ready to share exciting discoveries. When I ask, "Who has something to share?" most are so eager to participate that they can barely contain themselves. Amazing ideas pop out of their mouths, and children build on their classmates' thoughts to make their own discoveries. The room fills with a rich banter of questions, new learning, and a whole new world of words the kindergartners have never before expressed. Observers tend to watch and listen and then ask incredulously, "How do you *do* that?"

The answer is . . . very slowly. Back in August, my classroom looked quite different. Some children didn't know how to turn the pages of a book or even where to hang their coats. They eagerly but thoughtlessly groped classroom materials. One child might have been hitting a classmate who'd invaded his space or taken something from him; another child might have been sitting sullenly alone, talking to no one. Settling in means not just physically calming down but attempting to get past various kinds of emotional and behavioral issues, such as punching a friend, grabbing when you want something, and learning how to listen and follow directions. At the start of the school year, no matter how gently I asked or how much guidance I provided, questions like "Who has something to share?" yielded only blank looks or inarticulate grunts.

The road from the formless August classroom to November's well-oiled machine starts with three important words: *setting the tone*. Setting the tone for learning is a precise, deliberate process for any teacher. It takes time and thoughtful work to fine-tune a clear vision of what you value, what you want your students to value, and what you believe is best for them. What are the most important messages to communicate to children as they walk through the classroom door? What rituals and routines will set the stage and support learning for the rest of the day, or the year? Kindergartners thrive on routine, so what happens at the start is especially important.

I teach at Harrington Elementary, a K–6 public school in the northeast section of Denver, ten minutes from downtown. Approximately three-quarters of our five hundred students are Hispanic; most of the rest are African American. All are eligible for free or reduced-price lunch. Roughly half my kindergartners come to school with preschool experience. The others have no experience at all with such basics as how to hang up a backpack, what tone of voice to use in a classroom, how to sit still, and how to hold a classroom pet, never mind experience with bigger issues like how to ask a question or communicate thoughts and feelings.

Harrington has no bells. Teachers pick up and dismiss their students at appropriate times throughout the day without the traditional reminders blaring from the intercom. Removing something as mundane as a bell makes the school feel much more civil and less institutional. But even without bells, I keep the kindergarten day highly organized. I value freedom of choice and very much want to help the students develop decision-making skills. But for kindergartners, it's important that freedom come within a framework of routine that they can learn and depend on. The comfort of ritual gives them the confidence to choose. Table 2–1 is a schedule of a typical week in my kindergarten class at Harrington.

For the last six years I've taught full-day kindergarten. In the nineteen years before that, when I taught two half-day sessions, I did writing and reading two days a week and math and choice (open time when students pick their activities) on two other days. Fridays were flexible, emphasizing writing, reading, math, art, cooking, or choice, depending on the needs of the children.

I implement our morning routine over the first month of school. The children spend this time learning the basics:

- expected classroom and school behaviors
- appropriate community etiquette (how to sit, listen, share, ask questions)

Time	Activity	
	TABLE 2-1 *Typical Kindergarten Schedule*	
	Monday–Thursday	*Friday*
8:10–8:35	Book checkout; independent reading	
8:35–9:10	Sharing; attendance; message board; songs on charts	
9:10–9:20	Movement	
9:20–10:25	Writing workshop read-aloud or modeled writing minilesson; independent practice; author's share	Drawing/art activity/cooking/ science/social studies/dry-erase board work—letter formation and penmanship in isolation or integrated with simple sight words (45 minutes); independent reading (30 minutes)
10:25–10:45	Snack; outdoor recess	
10:50–11:30	Reading workshop: songs; shared reading/minilesson; independent reading; reader's share	Shared reading/short story (10 minutes); music; rhythms (20 minutes)
11:30–12:15	Lunch	
12:20–12:40	Song; story	
12:40–1:25	Math workshop: minilesson; independent practice; math share	Math games: minilesson; independent practice; math share
1:25–2:10	Choice	
2:10–2:50	Specials (art, music, PE, computers, library—once a week)	
2:50–3:00	Songs; acknowledgments	
3:00	Dismissal	

- routines (book checkout, independent reading, morning songs, attendance, and calendar rituals)
- uses of various areas of the classroom
- initial logistics of a writing and reading workshop (how to get to and from writing tables, arrangement of books, etc.)

I introduce new components to the schedule gradually, while carefully reviewing behavioral expectations.

■ Settling In

In the mornings, my kindergartners stream into the school, hanging coats and back-packs in the hallway. As they enter the classroom, I greet each child with a hug and a steady flow of conversation and reminders.

"Good morning! Good job, sweetheart, you remembered your checkout book."

"Did Mom read your book? . . . What do you think—did you like it? . . . Go tell a friend how much you enjoyed it; she might want to check it out."

Children smile as they hunt around the room for Floppy the bunny, who's hop-ping about. They pass the homes of Cajita the box turtle and Rosie the tarantula as they head to the checkout shelf to return their books. After finding their name card on the "Who is absent?" board, they place it in the can marked "I am here today!"

If they have remembered to bring back their book from the preceding day, they check out a new one by signing their name on a library card from inside the book and putting the card in their book checkout pocket, located near the cubbies. A close-up photograph of each child is glued to each checkout pocket, just above the name. This helps minimize any confusion in finding the correct pocket and adds a warm smile to anyone who passes by (see Figure 2–1).

Classroom book checkout is part of the children's daily homework. I am proud to say that 95 percent of my kindergartners are read to by someone in their house-hold every day. "Reading is the single most important thing you can do to help your child become a better reader," I constantly tell parents. If a student consis-tently neglects to return books to school, I phone the parents and speak about the importance of this daily ritual and their obligation in supporting their child's success.

After selecting a new book for homework, children spread out in the classroom and read quietly by themselves, or with partners on the carpet, as the rest of class set-tles in. Some read *Zoobooks* magazines, discovering great things about the world from the pictures, while others have a large book or songbook spread out on the floor (see Figure 2–2).

Cesar has the calendar job this week, so he's busy reading the days of the week and turning over the appropriate card. He puts up the current date and places the "Yesterday," "Today," and "Tomorrow" cards into the proper pockets (see Figure 2–3). Akeri, who has the weather job, is singing to the tune of "Skip to My Lou" while pointing to the words on a clipboard: "Hey, hey what do you say? Hey, hey what do you say? Hey, hey what do you say? For today's a sunny day" (see Figure 2–4). After

FIGURE 2–1 *Anahi checks out a classroom book.*

FIGURE 2–2 *My kindergartners settle in first thing in the morning.*

FIGURE 2–3 *Cesar positions "Yesterday," "Today," and "Tomorrow" cards in our calendar.*

finishing the song, she draws the weather on a little white square and adds it to the weather graph, hanging next to the calendar.

In the first weeks of the school year, the children do these jobs together as a class. After that, the jobs rotate, and I provide support as needed. This structure allows me to be individually engaged with one child while building independence in the others by allowing them choice and responsibility. Once children have acquired a skill such as the calendar, they don't need the daily support of the community; reinforcement is more effective and empowering when they perform tasks individually. Many times, when a child is doing a particular job, others in the vicinity are naturally drawn into his work and thus learn vicariously, providing additional opportunities for reinforcement.

Children who don't have specific jobs on any given day are free to do their own reading for the first twenty-five minutes. Today, Giovanni is sitting on the floor alone, so intent on studying a *Zoobooks* magazine that his body is curled around it.

"So what are you discovering, Giovanni?" I ask, looking over his shoulder at a photograph of the inside of a chicken egg.

FIGURE 2–4 *Akeri sings the weather song.*

"I don't know," he says.

"What do you think you are looking at? Look at the animal over here," I say, pointing to a fluffy chick on the right side of the page. "What could this be? Do you see that what you are looking at is the inside of something?"

He nods in agreement and doubtfully guesses, "A baby chick?"

"Yes, that's exactly what you are looking at!"

"Can I share?" he asks excitedly.

"Sure, bring it to the oval."

This settling-in time establishes the tone for the day. Right away, as children enter the classroom, they can understand what our community values: reading, thinking, questioning, choice, and thoughtfully following through with independent tasks.

■ Oval Time

At 8:35 on a crisp October morning, I turn off the classroom lights, gently signaling the children to freeze and look at me. "Boys and girls, please put your books away with their titles facing out and join us on the oval." All of my little ones scatter about,

FIGURE 2–5 *The class gathers on the oval to share.*

returning books and magazines to their proper tubs or racks, and proceed to sit on the oval with legs crossed. Many have *Zoobooks* magazines open in front of them, eager to share a discovery (see Figure 2–5).

We spend the first three weeks of school learning about the importance of books: book arrangement in the classroom, proper handling of books, and the best behaviors for listening and reading. Only after this foundation is set do we proceed to *content* routines like how to read pictures, formulate questions, and share discoveries.

Our sharing space is specifically designed in the shape of an oval so that everyone can see and acknowledge the child who is sharing. (Our room's size didn't allow for a circle; thus, the oval, created with dashes of strapping tape stuck to the carpet.) When children are on the oval, they listen intently to one another, asking questions and expressing their thoughts at appropriate times. I teach them to share without raising their hands. Of course, enthusiastically sharing an idea is different from shouting over someone else's words, and establishing this balance requires delicate work by the teacher. I've found that my own practice of active engagement—speaking when I hear something meaningful—sets the model for the group. I do ask children to raise their hands at certain times, for example, when answering questions after a read-aloud.

"So who has something to share?" I ask. Giovanni's hand shoots up; he wants the class to know what he's discovered. "Do you know what you call this?" he asks the group, showing the picture of the inside of an egg. Silence.

I chime in. "Does anyone know what you call a growing or developing chick?"

Uvaldo, who is repeating kindergarten with me, hesitates and then shouts out, "Embryo!" (For the last fifteen years, I have incubated chick and duck eggs in the spring as a comparison study.)

"Wow, good remembering, Uvaldo! You're absolutely right. It doesn't look like a baby chick, so you can't call it a baby chick. It's called an *embryo*. Can all of you say that? *Embryo*." The children echo my language. "Do you know what you call that thing attached to the embryo?" I'm trying to elicit the words *yolk sack* (which I sense they wouldn't know).

Jared enthusiastically shouts out, "A cord, just like babies!"

Surprised, I say to him, "Wow, how did you know that?" honoring his thinking.

"Ms. Natalie read that to me!" Ms. Natalie is my paraprofessional in class.

"Good for you! I'm so glad you remembered the name," I tell Jared. And then to the class: "Jared's right; that thing attached to the embryo is called a cord. Do you know what you call the yellowish-orange stuff that's attached to the cord?" Blank stares. "What does it look like?"

Brayshon responds, "Egg."

"Good job. What *part* of an egg?"

I prompt everyone with a *yuh* sound, and several of the kids say, "Yolk!"

"Yes, that cord from the embryo is attached to this thing called a *yolk sack*. Can all of you say *yolk sack*? Does anyone know what this yolk sack is for?"

Uvaldo, remembering details from last year, responds, "Food."

"Yes, that yolk sack is food for the developing embryo. The embryo sucks up the yolk to get its food, just as you suck milk from a straw." As I share, I make sucking sounds and emulate holding a straw, as a way to anchor this new information. They all mimic my movement and sucking sound. Movement and echoing words or sounds are common classroom rituals. Children have a far better chance of retaining information that's delivered with kinesthetic or auditory components.

The share continues. Passion has discovered that pandas slide down hills on their tummies, much the way children do. I read from the caption of the picture she found that scientists have actually seen pandas climbing back up the hill for a second run. "So, just like children, what do pandas like to do?"

"Play!" they all enthusiastically respond.

Stomp, Trumpet, Learn

Brayshon has a *Zoobooks* magazine spread before him and his hand raised, ready to share. "Brayshon, did you discover something?"

"Elephant . . . dirt . . . dust," are the only words he can manage as he shows the picture.

"What are you noticing, Brayshon? What do you mean, *elephant dust*? What is the elephant doing?" He stares at me, not knowing how to respond. I prompt, "How do you think he is making that dust?"

"Walking. His feet!"

"OK. But wait a minute, Brayshon, is the elephant just *walking* to make this dust?" Several kids shout out, "No, he's stomping!"

"Wow, what a great *rich* word. *Stomping*! Yeah, that's exactly what elephants do. They stomp their feet in the dry dirt and create dust all around them."

As I share this information, I stand up and act out the motions so that the children can see and hear what the elephants do. Then I segue back to Brayshon. "Brayshon, can you say, 'Elephants stomp their feet to make dust'?" Brayshon requires language support. In this case, he is fully comprehending what he's heard but can't articulate his thinking in a complete thought. I need to break the sentence into smaller chunks so that he can echo my words accurately. Taking time to develop and expand language is critical work for young children (Paynter, Bodrova, and Doty 2005).

After Brayshon has repeated the sentence, I ask the group, "Does anyone know why an elephant would want to create all that dust?"

Reysean (*RAY-shon*), Munira (*MOO-neer-ah*), and Robert shout out, "Read those words!" By this time in the school year, the children know the purpose of captions.

"Oh, good thinking! You mean the writing beside the photograph, called a *caption*? You're so smart!"

"Yeah!" they say.

"Well, it says, 'Although an elephant's skin is thick . . .' Do you guys know what *thick* means?" They stare with blank looks. "*Thick* means . . . like . . . if you had a thick sandwich, you would have lots of cheese, meat, tomatoes, and lettuce between two slices of bread."

Oops. I wince at my own analogy. The minute you mention food of any sort to kindergartners, it is all they can think about. At least half the group instantly starts saying, "Yum! Yum!" or "I don't like cheese," or "Ick! Tomatoes!"

As I describe this large sandwich, I anchor the word by separating my hands and showing *thick*. "Can all of you show me a thick sandwich and say *thick*?" All of the children spread their hands much too far apart for a realistic sandwich, but that doesn't matter; they understand the concept. "If this is *thick*, can you show me *thin*?" I demonstrate *thin* with my hands slightly separated, anchoring the vocabulary.

"Now let's go back and reread the caption and see if this makes sense. OK, it says:

> Although an elephant's skin is thick, it doesn't have a "tough hide." Instead, its one- to one-and-a-half-inch skin is extremely sensitive. To protect itself from biting insects, sunburn, and skin disease, an elephant bathes fre-

quently, sprays dust on its skin, and rolls in mud, which dries into a thick coat of muddy "armor."

"Wow, so that means that even though an elephant's skin is really *thick* [again emphasizing the word with my hands], it still can feel those pesky insects biting! Elephants create dust all around them in order to get rid of the bugs flying around them. That's really neat! Hmm, so when elephants get itchy, they don't reach around the back with their trunk and scratch themselves?"

"No!" the kids respond, giggling.

"Can all of you guys stand up and stomp around like elephants?"

Whenever they have a chance to move, the students jump instantly to their feet. I intentionally incorporate movement in context throughout the day, both to anchor new concepts and language kinesthetically and to let the kids get their wiggles out. Movement taps the emotional and creative domains and gives comprehension another context in which to live. Children who can link learning through several kinds of sensory experiences have a far better chance of retaining information (Fauth 1990).

"Wait a second. Before you start, I want you to visualize—picture yourself—as a great big elephant, surrounded by a bunch of nasty biting flies. I want you to stomp your feet, creating lots of dust, so you can get rid of all those pesky insects that are flying around. Can you *feel* the dust flying? Can you *see* it? Let me hear you trumpet like elephants. Wow, great job! Try to see and feel all those insects flying away from you."

All of the children and I are stomping around the oval loudly, making trumpeting sounds. "Boy, I feel much better now!" I say in my best elephant voice. "Can all my little elephants sit back down on the oval?" Once the children are seated on their bottoms, with legs crossed and voices off, we continue our share.

It Starts with a Question

"You know, Giovanni, I was thinking about the question you were writing about the other day: Why do monkeys ride on the backs of elephants?" Giovanni had noticed monkeys sitting on the backs of elephants in a *Zoobooks* magazine he was reading, and I had suggested that he record his discovery. With minimal support, he wrote about it (see Figure 2–6).

Here's how that writing came to be: using questioning as a comprehension strategy, I had asked Giovanni if he wondered anything about the elephant and the monkey. Initially, he didn't respond. That's common when you introduce the thinking strategy *questioning*: a child will look at you, not quite comprehending what you want. Now, on the oval, I want to remind Giovanni and the other students that many of our questions start with close observation. "Remember in that book we were just reading, *Why Is the Sky Blue?* Rabbit learned so much about the world from

FIGURE 2–6 *Giovanni's writing:* I learned that monkeys ride on elephants' backs! Why? They want to see the whole [wide] world!

just looking closely. Does anyone remember that rich word that means to look closely?"

The kids enthusiastically respond, "Observing!" The children know this language because they have heard me use it so often in context. At the beginning of the year, I spend time modeling and emphasizing the importance of observation. I encourage children to frequently observe Houdinni, our garter snake; Rosie, our tarantula; Cajita, our box turtle; Fire and Jumpy, our fire-bellied toads; Floppy, our mini lop; Swimmer, our water turtle; and all the fish in our aquarium. All of us continually talk and share with others what we notice and discover; so much is learned by watching closely.

"That's right! Rabbit was slowing down and taking time to observe. If he had never stopped and looked closely to observe the spots on the ladybugs, would he have ever known that some ladybugs have two spots, some have five, some have seven, or some have six?"

"No!" the kids respond.

"You're absolutely right. If he had never taken the time and paid attention to detail, he would never have known that ladybugs have different numbers of spots on them. That's the great gift that Rabbit gave to Donkey! He taught Donkey to stop, look closely, and . . ."

The children finish my thought enthusiastically: "Observe!"

"That's just what you did, Giovanni, when you were reading that *Zoobooks* magazine on elephants. You didn't just flip through the magazine quickly; you were carefully looking at the illustration of the monkey on the back of the elephant. Lots of times, our questions come from just observing. At first, you didn't wonder about the monkeys; you were just *discovering* that they ride on the backs of elephants. Then I shared with you that *I* was wondering why the monkey was on top of the elephant. You seemed interested in that question and wanted to ask it yourself."

When children share their discoveries, I always share something that I authentically wonder about. By modeling questioning, I'm giving them implied permission not to know all the answers. (If I knew the answer, then why would I ask the question?) My question must be a real one because children immediately sense what's authentic. The more they see and feel your investment in their thinking, the more engaged and serious they become with their own learning.

When Giovanni first shared his discovery on the oval several days earlier, he hadn't yet progressed from discovering to wondering. So I simply said to him, "Why? I'm wondering *why* monkeys ride on the backs of elephants." I honestly wanted to know. Why did the publishers of *Zoobooks* include this picture of a monkey on the back of an elephant? There must be a reason, and I certainly didn't know it.

As soon as I shared my thinking with Giovanni, he looked at me and said, "Yeah, how come?"

"I don't know, sweetheart. You might want to write about what you're wondering today." A huge smile spread across his face as he nodded. "Picture yourself as a monkey way on top of an elephant, and think about why you would want to be there," I suggested. He giggled. You could almost see the wheels turning in his head as I left him with the thought.

So much of what children write is what they talk about. The things children choose to share are their most pressing thoughts in the moment: a loose tooth, sparkly new shoes, feeling sad because their mom yelled at them or a friend called them a name. It is critical that we listen to their dialogue and link those thoughts to print. Children's talk is the seeds for the stories they write.

During writing time, I supported Giovanni with vocabulary to stretch out his observation and question. He was more than ready to do this work independently, but he tends to struggle with confidence. The following day at writing time, I encouraged him toward the next step. "You may not know the answer to your question, Giovanni, and that's OK. I want you to think what the very best answer to your wondering might be and write that down on the back of your question. Think about yourself as a monkey. Why might you want to be up there on top of the elephant?" I left him alone after planting this question, and Giovanni proceeded to do just as I'd asked.

Midway through our writing workshop, I asked, "Did you finish your best thinking?" He nodded. "Good job, honey!" I said, approaching his table. "Can you read to me what you wrote?"

I was so proud of him as he read what he had independently written: "TheAW-toCTheHWrLD!" (*They want to see the whole world!*). When he read it aloud, he actually said, "They want to see the whole *wide* world!" This was what he intended to communicate, so those were the words I echoed.

"They want to see the whole wide world. What a great answer to your question. I love it!" He beamed as I put my arm around him and squeezed his shoulder gently.

"Can I share in the author's chair?" he asked enthusiastically.

"Absolutely!"

Eat Bugs, Connect Discoveries

Now, sitting in the oval with the group, I know that this experience from a few days earlier is still fresh in Giovanni's mind, so I draw him into Brayshon's discovery. "Giovanni, think about what Brayshon just discovered. Why do you think monkeys might ride on the backs of elephants?"

Giovanni quickly responds, "So they can see the whole wide world!"

"Yes, I love that answer! But do you have some other thoughts about why they might ride on elephants' backs?"

"No," he says, shaking his head.

"Do you remember when we were at the zoo last week?"

"Yeah!"

"Well, the kids in my group observed the monkeys doing something really interesting. James, Uvaldo, Brayshon, Reysean, do any of you guys remember what we saw?"

After several seconds of silence, Uvaldo blurts out, "They were eating bugs!"

"That's right! One monkey was picking the insects off another monkey and . . ."

All four boys finish my sentence, "Eating them!"

"*Ooh! Yuck!*" the rest of the class responds.

"That's disgusting!" several girls add.

"Well, it may seem gross to *people*, but that's just what monkeys do: they pick the insects out of one another's hair and eat them. That's called grooming."

A low murmur of "Ooh yuck" continues. Their faces contort in disgust as I ask, "Can you guys say *grooming*?" They reluctantly echo the word.

"Uvaldo, come out here in the middle of the oval and pretend you're a monkey grooming me." He shoots me a look as if to ask whether I could possibly be serious. "Come on, Uvaldo, I've got a lot of insects living in my hair. I need you to get them out! They're itching me!"

The rest of the children giggle, their eyes riveted on the two of us in the center of the oval. I sit flat on the floor, interspersing monkey grunts, while Uvaldo simulates plucking insects. "Uvaldo, what do you need to do with them once you pick them out of my hair?"

He stares at me before reluctantly responding, "Eat them."

"Yes, honey. You can't just pick them out. You've got to *eat them*!"

In the middle of this demonstration, I ask, "Giovanni, do have any more thoughts about why monkeys might want to ride on the backs of elephants?" He shakes his head, smiling. I want to make sure he has gone as deep as he can with his thinking, so I ask, "You don't? Are you sure?" I give him a long wait time, but he sticks with the *no*. "Well," I say as Uvaldo continues to forage in my hair, "I'm thinking maybe monkeys like to be way on top because . . . what's flying around the elephant?"

"Insects!" the kids respond.

James can barely contain himself at this point, and shouts out, "'Cause they wanna eat those bugs!"

"Yeah! I think they might like to sit up there so they can eat insects. What could be better than having your tummy filled and getting to see the whole wide world at the same time! I don't know . . . ," I say, leaving them with this dangling thought. The children all giggle at this notion. "You know if we really wanted to find out why they ride on the backs of elephants, what would we need to do?"

I prompt them with *Re-ser*, and together they chime in unison, "Research!"

I encourage students to do their own research when questions arise. Sometimes they can find the answer with the resources in our room, but if not, they head to the library with question in hand to be supported by our media specialist. Other times, I do Internet research on my own and bring the information back to the class.

So, for example, Alicia's question "HOW Do aNTS MoHCH iN A STsDT LiN?" (*How do ants march in a straight line?*) was generated from observing ants as they marched across a log in her aunt's backyard. This prompted her to perform research with our librarian, and she returned to class with *Those Amazing Ants* (Demuth 1994) in hand. The answer to her research can be seen in Figure 2–7.

■ Establishing a Culture of Purposeful Learning

In any conversation I have with children, I'm attuned to the three domains, which are always present but shift between foreground and background depending on the circumstance. For example, Giovanni's experiences involved the cognitive domain when he was asking questions; the creative domain when he was sharing his new learning; and the emotional domain in all those moments when feelings of doubt, excitement, or pride surfaced.

FIGURE 2–7 *Alicia's research results:* Ants smell food! They let tiny droplets out from the tummy!

Context is everywhere; it shapes our attempts to make meaning of the world. Usually we operate from several contexts at the same time without being aware of them. But for students and teachers, understanding contexts and how they're layered is essential to comprehension.

Classrooms abound with context; the trick in teaching is to layer them deliberately. When I call everyone into the oval and ask the students to talk and share discoveries, we've created contexts of community and sharing that affect both the individual and the group. If someone brings up a question about animals from a science book, that establishes the context not just of science but of literacy (using language to talk about language). When I ask children to mimic sounds, or I physically demonstrate the meaning of a word, the context of movement adds another layer of comprehension. A structure built of multiple contexts forms a powerful system of learning.

Conversely, stripping away contexts diminishes learning. In Giovanni's share, for example, if you took away the context of movement, you would remove an insightful layer of understanding: Reenacting the sucking sounds of the embryo absorbing the yolk helped the children gain a better understanding of what happens inside an egg. If you took away the context of science, the entire discussion of the embryo and yolk would not have surfaced; Giovanni would simply have shared an illustration of the inside of an egg.

If you took away the context of literacy, the children would never have developed rich vocabulary such as *embryo* and *yolk*. If you took away the context of sharing, only one child would have benefited from the information. And if you took away the context of community, Giovanni would have been wondering alone, unable to figure out the meaning of *embryo*. He would have been left with an unexplained image, and the rest of the children would have missed out on this new learning as well. Together, all the contexts—movement, science, literacy, sharing, and community—shaped the meaning of *embryo*, creating a greater radius of learning for Giovanni and every student in the class.

When a child shares on the oval, she is contributing to the learning community. Stories and thoughts embedded in memory are gently coaxed out and developed so that they can be expressed in words. Language is enhanced; learning is clarified. Everyone benefits. Our morning talk on the oval provides generous opportunities for children to share thoughts and discoveries; it creates a safe, nurturing, predictable space for learning. During these conversations, we spend much time developing and extending oral language because so many skills—developing language, building and accessing schema (background knowledge on a given topic), reasoning critically, questioning—directly relate to a child's ability to comprehend text.

Thoughts developed during these talks become the stories children write. This is where language comes full circle. A child begins with a thought, expresses it verbally, and links that thought through writing to the printed page. Eventually, kindergartners come to see the process this way:

> What we *think*, we can *say*.
> What we *say*, we can *write*.
> What we *write*, we can *read*.

As teachers of literacy, we continually connect thinking with spoken and written words.

Vocabulary knowledge is the single most important indicator of a child's success with reading (Laflamme 1997). Children who are at risk often start school already disadvantaged in exposure to language, as compared with their middle-class counterparts. As Hart and Risley point out, these children simply have not heard as many words:

> The average child on welfare was having half as much experience per hour (616 words per hour) as the average working-class child (1,251 words per hour) and less than one-third that of the average child in a professional

family (2,153 words per hour). . . . By age 4, the average child in a welfare family might have 13 million fewer words of cumulative experience than the average child in a working-class family. (Hart and Risley 2003)

Because of this disparity, I spend most of my year developing language and providing rich experiences to enhance background knowledge. I look for chances to anchor language and information through movement. Children love being able to get up and act something out; why not capitalize on their natural inclinations? The action not only gives them a cognitive break but substantially increases their ability to retain pertinent information. As Howard Gardner stated:

> The brain learns best and retains most when the organism is actively involved in exploring physical sites and materials and asking questions to which it actually craves answers. Merely passive experiences tend to attenuate and have little lasting impact. (1999, 82)

When children reenact an elephant's stomp in the dust to rid itself of flies, they are creating new mental constructs kinesthetically, expanding their knowledge base (creative domain) while strengthening their sense of self (emotional domain). When they discuss their discoveries in a group, they are strengthening their own voices and taking ownership of their learning. Sharing strengthens the class individually and collectively, setting the precedent that we are all teachers and learners.

From the first day of the school year, everything I do in the classroom aims to create a tight community built of respect, love, and support, one where children's natural wonder and excitement become routes to learning. By giving children a predictable time to clarify ideas, articulate thoughts, and explore questions about themselves and the world, I am strengthening these skills within them. I want school to enhance, not squelch, children's passion for discovery, to provide them with new eyes for viewing the world and new tools for making sense of it.

■ Where to Start

- Reflect on the tone you set for the day. Does it match your beliefs and values for learning?
- Identify your classroom rituals and routines. Do they make your beliefs and values explicit?
- Keep a journal of classroom experiences. Watch children carefully and listen to their language. At what point were you seeing opportunities to enter the different domains? How did you take advantage of those or, in retrospect, how *could* you have?

3 | Integrated Learning

When we try to pick out anything by itself, we find it hitched to everything else in the Universe.

—John Muir

"Yellow! Brown! White! Green! Yellow! Brown! White! Green!"

The rhythmic chanting of children's voices must have sounded mysterious to anyone passing by my classroom one mid-October afternoon.

"Yellow! Brown! White! Green!"

Peering into the room would only have deepened the mystery. There I was, sitting with the children on the oval, pointing to colored cubes linked in order as all of us chanted intently: "Yellow! Brown! White! Green!" But we weren't using just our voices; within seconds we were on our feet, moving our hands and our whole bodies in time with the color names: "Yellow [hand clap]! Brown [finger snap]! White [jump]! Green [wiggle]! Yellow [clap]! Brown [snap]! White [jump]! Green [wiggle]!"

Children were jumping, children were wiggling, and any minute now they were going to figure out that our chant had something to do with the seasons we'd talked about that morning. All of this was happening because of a rainbow—and none of it was what I'd expected to be doing when I arrived at school that morning.

■ Connected Learning

Teaching kindergarten requires the flexibility of a yoga instructor, or maybe Gumby. When things are going well, you feel like the conductor of a well-rehearsed miniature orchestra. But we kindergarten teachers know that our true mission is much messier, much more like jazz improvisation than chamber music. Integrating learning—surrounding children with it from all directions, offering myriad ways for them to discover and understand—requires a unique combination of laser focus and something much more difficult: trusting yourself to go with the flow. You keep your eyes and ears open. You follow where the children lead. You look for connections. You find ways to make it all come together.

When I was a child, my learning was fragmented. I didn't understand, and was never shown, how information fits together into a cohesive whole. So when I became a teacher, I desperately wanted to do better for my students. I started training myself to slow down and really think about how each concept I taught might fit with concepts in other lessons, past or present.

No one is born knowing how to make these connections in the classroom, and in my early years of teaching, I didn't even realize it was possible. In those days, thematic units were the rage. When the subject was bears, for example, bears were everywhere: We read books about bears, made a cut-and-paste art project about bears, sang songs about bears, did math problems involving bears. We topped off the unit with a teddy bear picnic, for which students brought their stuffed animals to school. "Wow," I thought, "I'm really integrating my curriculum." But gradually I came to realize that although the connections looked great on the surface, that's the only place they existed. Thematic units lacked depth and breadth. When we finished a unit, we moved on, as if a linear progression of topics were the complete definition of education.

Thematic units left no space for children to take the lead, following their interests and curiosity or spiraling back to build on previous knowledge. I knew I valued a different model even before I came to redefine the term *integrated learning* for myself. Other teachers use the phrase in different ways, but for me, integrated learning means connecting ideas, information, and experiences minute by minute, day by day, every day of the school year. It means analyzing your lesson plans to make sure the activities *matter*; they're not just time fillers or meaningless cutting and pasting.

Once I let go of thematic units, my teaching became much more exciting and more real. Now I listen for, and draw out, opportunities to show relationships. Everything in the world is related. Martin Luther King Jr. knew it when he said, "Whatever affects one directly, affects all indirectly." By making these connections visible from moment to moment, I model and promote synthesis in small and large increments. Eventually, a child's thinking will shift, but often in a small way, not as a huge *aha*. The more children understand interrelatedness, the more they can make their own connections, see practical applications of their learning, and begin to understand the world.

Though I always have an overall plan of instruction, I stay flexible within that structure so that I can follow where the children lead and capitalize on teachable moments. Even in a public school with a structured curriculum, teachers usually have flexibility in *how* they cover the material. Thus, when Ragat (*Rah-GOT*) asked one day, "Why is the sun bigger than the earth?" of course I didn't say, "That's a science question and this is reading time, so ask it later." That kind of response not only stunts a child's curiosity but discounts the way children see the world as one big, fascinating whole.

If a child asks about something that would take too long to address fully, I give a simplified explanation and defer the more detailed discussion until later. The process becomes a rich dance, with the children's questions and discoveries circling and interweaving like the many colors and textures of a tapestry. My job is to help them see the connections between their ideas and other children's ideas or between their ideas and something we've read or discussed before. Once I started listening to my students and helping them weave this tapestry, my job became not so much director of learning as facilitator. The shift has made a huge difference in the lenses through which I view teaching—and in how much I enjoy it.

Chapter 2 showed how it's possible to weave one child's question (Why do monkeys ride on the backs of elephants?) and another child's discovery (Elephants stomp their feet, creating dust, to rid themselves of insects) together with observations made on a field trip (Monkeys groom each other by plucking insects out of each other's fur and eating them). By listening carefully and identifying relationships among the various elements, I guided the conversation, helping not just Giovanni and Brayshon but the whole community connect separate pieces of information from different days to form a cohesive whole. The children's thoughts led all of us where none of us knew we'd be going.

■ The Four Seasons: Integrating the Curriculum

The rainbow on the wall that greeted my students that October morning was definitely something they'd seen before. At the start of the school year, when we'd first noticed that the water prism in our east window was creating a rainbow high on the west wall, everyone had questions: What makes a rainbow? Why do we have one in our room? We talked about water, sun, and reflections. We used movement to explore how prisms work, breaking our hands apart to show the light's colors separating, then pulling them back together to represent white light.

On this fall day, however, some students noticed that the rainbow looked different. Not only had it moved from high on the west wall to lower on the north wall, but it had gotten smaller and its colors had faded. The morning share on the oval started with a spirited discussion about why the rainbow had moved and why it seemed to be staying with us for a shorter time each day. The students were leading me: they were ready to learn more about the seasons.

With help from our globe, I demonstrated how our planet slowly revolves around the sun. At different times of the year, the earth tilts closer or farther away from this hot ball. As the earth slowly turns and leans, the sun shines down on us in different spots. "What season are we in right now?" I asked, knowing that most of my students didn't know the word *season*. They could describe what they did and saw at various times of the year, but they didn't have vocabulary to label those periods. "What do we call this time of the year?" The children gave me blank stares. "OK, then what season did we just finish? Remember the frozen pops?"

"Summer!" they shouted in unison.

"Yes, summer is a *season*, the time of year when the earth is closest to the sun.

"What does summer feel like? What can you do?"

"It's hot! You don't have to wear shoes!"

"Yeah! And after summer, the earth starts to lean away," I said, demonstrating with the globe again. "Then guess what happens to the temperature?"

"It goes down!"

"Yes, our days begin to cool off, and what do the leaves do?"

"Turn brown and fall!"

"Do you remember what season we call this?" They hesitated. "*Fff,*" I hinted.

"Fall!" several children shouted out.

"Yes, this season, or time of the year, is called *fall* or *autumn*. Can you guys say that?"

We reviewed the four seasons in sequence by reciting them together, raising one finger at a time to represent order. We repeated this cycle several times. "What do you notice?" I asked. "What do you call something that keeps happening over and over?"

"A pattern!" they confidently blurted out.

"Yes! Well, summer just ended, so what season are we in again?"

Almost the entire class responded, "Fall!"

"That's right. Because the earth is moving, the sun is shining down in a different place, so now when the light shines through the window, it hits the water prism at a different spot than it used to. That's why our rainbow has moved. On your first day of school, it was summer, and the sun was shining over there and making a rainbow high up on that other wall. That summer rainbow used to stay most of the morning, remember?

"Now the rainbow has moved to another wall, and it stays for only a short while. By the time you finish checking out books, the rainbow has left our classroom for the rest of the day.

"Where does the sun go after it shines through our window?" No response.

"Remember, the sun rises . . . where?" The children pointed toward the windows. "What direction do we call that?"

"East!"

"Good remembering! The sun rises in the east. Do you remember the rich word that describes the time of morning when the sun comes up? It starts *Ddd* . . ."

The children responded, "Dawn!"

"Yes. Then it slowly rises and says hello to us, and then what?"

"It goes up in the sky!"

"Yeah! What time of the day is it when the sun is directly above us?"

"Lunch!"

As I reviewed the positions of the sun, we all used American Sign Language (ASL) to sign the sunrise as we faced east, then continued until we were facing west and signing night, with the sun setting.

"So what do you think will happen to the rainbow in the winter?" I asked.

A few of the children said, "It's gonna go away."

"We'll have to watch it very closely," I said.

"But maybe it will come back in the spring!" Auriyah (*ARE-e-yah*) interjected.

"Great thinking, Auriyah! I think you might be right. We'll have to wait and see."

I knew this was a discussion we would return to, revisiting learning. When children are given opportunities to explore and reexamine concepts, they comprehend them on a deeper level.

Knowing my classroom library and its organization, I quickly grabbed *Round and Round the Seasons Go* (Williams 1994d) from one of the songbook tubs, and we all started singing, "Round and round the seasons go, winter comes, cold white snow. Round and round the seasons go, spring comes, flowers grow . . . ," to the tune of "London Bridge Is Falling Down."

Later in the day as we sat in the oval during our math minilesson, I asked the children to observe closely as I linked together four colors of plastic cubes into one long strand. Several eager hands shot up and as children called out, "A pattern!"

"Great noticing. Let's read it by color." Starting on the left and moving to the right, reinforcing left-to-right progression in reading, I pointed my finger to each cube as we collectively recited the colors, "Yellow, brown, white, green. Yellow, brown, white, green."

Recognizing and reproducing patterns is an essential kindergarten skill. Because patterns are one of the basic underlying concepts of math, children need to understand them before they can take on such areas as numeration and symmetry. Patterns also have numerous applications to science and literature. For example, listening to a song and recognizing the repeated chorus or hearing a story and predicting expected language fosters verbal fluency. Noticing the darkened gray clouds, predicting a rainstorm, and knowing the sun will show its bright face later, only to repeat this cyclical pattern, gives a child great confidence and a deeper understanding of his world.

"Can we clap and snap the pattern this time?" I asked. When reading patterns kinesthetically, it helps to begin with the same movements for the first two colors or shapes every time. Over the years, clap and snap have become my two constant first movements. As patterns become more sophisticated, it's easier to recall the movements associated with the colors or shapes when the first two are always the same; this is especially true when the length of the pattern is extended to six, seven, or eight items.

That's why we started the color chant with *yellow* (clap) and *brown* (snap). Then I asked the group, "What movement should we do on white?"

"Let's jump!" several children shouted.

"Great! What should we do on green?"

"Wiggle your body," Toneeshia suggested.

"I like that. Great! Can all of you stand up and wiggle your body like Toneeshia, and say *green*? Good job!"

As always, we collectively read and moved to the pattern three or four times, to allow everyone to anchor it kinesthetically. Then, as everyone sat back down on the oval, I nudged the children's thinking further by asking, "Can any of you read this pattern by what the colors remind you of? Think about the seasons we talked about this morning. What season might yellow remind you of? Think about what season brown could be. In what season would you see a lot of white? Think about in what season you see lots of green."

These questions pushed them to an abstract level of thinking, associating seasons with colors. Encouraging children to read patterns on many different levels (colors, shapes, associations) helps them generalize later to many content areas. As I planted these seeds, I could almost see the wheels turning in their little heads.

"Yellow, like summer, 'cause it's really hot!" Auriyah called enthusiastically.

"Good job! What season do you think brown could be? What's happening to the leaves?"

"They're all turning brown and falling off the trees!" Tajanee (*TAH-jah-nay*) shouted.

"Great! What season do you call this?"

"Fall!"

"How about white?"

In unison, several children yelled out, "Winter!"

"You guys are really thinking! What season does green remind you of?" There was a moment of silence. "Think about what season it is when everything starts to turn green and grow."

"Spring!" they enthusiastically chimed in.

"OK, let's read the pattern by seasons this time."

Once again, my finger tracked the colored blocks from left to right as we collectively recited the pattern in a different way: "Summer, fall, winter, spring. Summer, fall, winter, spring."

"Why don't we try putting a movement with each season?"

"Yeah!" the children chimed in enthusiastically.

"What could we do for the hot sun we feel in summer?"

"Make a big ball!"

"Great! How about the brown for fall?" The children stared quietly at me. "What's happening to the leaves?"

"They're falling off!"

"What could we do with our fingers?" I asked. Several children immediately fluttered their fingers in a downward movement, simulating the leaves falling. "I love that! Let's all try that and say *fall* at the same time. Now what should we do for winter?" Several kids instantly crossed their arms and clutched their bodies while saying, "Brrr."

"That's great; I love it! And what movement should we do for spring?" The room remained quiet. I looked over at Alicia, who signed *grow* with her hands. "Wow, Alicia, that's perfect for spring! Let's put it all together."

The children and I read the pattern collectively, adding the movements to anchor the sequential order of the seasons:

summer (arms forming a large ball to represent the sun)
fall (fingers fluttering downward)
winter (clutching ourselves and saying, "Brr!")
spring (using the ASL sign for *grow*)

We repeated the pattern a few times and then again, this time replacing *fall* with *autumn* to expand vocabulary.

Two days later on a gorgeous fall day, our class took a wonderful field trip to the Denver Zoo. As my small group headed toward the pachyderm house, Malicah observed the brown, yellow, and reddish leaves falling gently from the branches of the tree. "Look, Mrs. Kempton," she said with a great big smile. "It's fall!" And her fingers fluttered in a downward motion.

■ What We Can Learn

By explicitly demonstrating connections, teachers help students perceive information as meaningful. Integrating learning deepens comprehension and retention, develops critical thinking, provides opportunities for synthesis, and promotes discovery. Learning becomes dynamic when children make their own connections. So like all the best parts of teaching, integration comes from listening to students. I hadn't expected to move from the rainbow to the seasons that day in October, but the children's observations made it a natural progression; they gave me the idea of pulling in the songbook and the concept of pattern. Even so, it didn't occur to me until later that I could reinforce the lesson further during math time, by showing the season pattern as a never-ending cycle. I was excited about making these new connections, so no wonder the kids were excited too.

Integrated learning is a process of determining importance through listening, eliminating extraneous material, connecting information and skills, and making instruction precise. Students aren't the only ones who benefit. Viewing education holistically has strengthened my own critical thinking skills; it's helped me find opportunities for synthesis as much as it's helped my students. Most of all, integrated learning has helped me trust my students and myself.

I measure children's ability to integrate learning by looking at their participation in an inquiry. If they recognize a relationship before I mention it, I know they're starting to take charge of their education. Often I'll be talking about something with a child when she'll excitedly blurt out, "That's just like . . . !" Then the child will run and get a book or magazine we've read to validate her thinking about connections.

The story of the rainbow didn't end in October. Sure enough, as Auriyah had astutely predicted, our classroom rainbow reappeared in the spring, large and bright on our west wall. We again revisited our learning, reviewing the science and math concepts associated with the seasons.

▧ Integrated Learning in Morning Rituals

The following sections are brief snippets illustrating how I integrate song, music, reading, and math skills in the course of our morning.

Tracking Charted Songs: Integrating Music, Oral Language, and Reading

One of our morning rituals is singing songs or chants, usually accompanied by recorded music. The words hang clipped and laminated on a chart stand, centrally located in the classroom, and have been brightly illustrated by the children and me. As the year progresses, I add new lyrics to our repertoire and rotate favorite songs, adding variety and choice. Smaller laminated versions of some of the songs and rhymes ("Days of the Week," "I'm a Rainbow," "One, Two, Bubblegum Chew") are placed in tubs labeled "Classroom Songs" and "Jump Rope Rhymes," where children can choose them during reading workshop. In addition, everyone is free to read the

FIGURE 3–1 *I support Akeri with her job as pointer.*

charted songs during independent reading time first thing in the morning and during choice time.

When we sing together as a class, one child has the job of "pointer," tracking words with a rhythm stick. The tracking provides another literacy context for children to learn about how print moves on a page, while simultaneously developing and strengthening language skills. I rotate the job to a different child every two weeks, rather than weekly, to allow each student sufficient experience (see Figure 3–1).

Music is strategically sprinkled throughout our daily rituals, giving depth and breadth to our classroom. As part of our greeting ritual in the morning, music calms the children and brings more focused energy to our community. The same is true for singing before reading workshop, after returning from the playground, or before leaving at the end of the day. Songs reinforce rituals and ease transitions.

All children crave song. The instant singing commences, children gaze up with loving, focused attention. We can capitalize on this seemingly innate attraction by integrating music with the context of reading. Singing songs, reciting well-known rhymes, and pointing to printed words not only develop language structures but also

FIGURE 3–2 *The children and I listen to music as we get ready to jump.*

reinforce basic concepts of print such as left-to-right movement, letter-sound associations, and functions of punctuation.

When children need a break from cognitive work, the music we play accompanies our movement, adding life, rhythm, and energy. Children love to request favorites: "Mrs. Kempton, can we do 'The Freeze' or 'The Dancing Machine?'" (Gregg and Steve classics) or "I wanna do 'See How I'm Jumping!'" (see Figure 3–2).

At the beginning of the year, when children are adjusting to a full-day school schedule, lullabies soothe the mood. During writing workshop, soft instrumental tunes play as background to facilitate children's focus. During stressful times or at the end of the school year, I turn off the lights as students lie on the carpet, in their own space, and listen to soothing tunes or to my voice singing "Hush Little Baby" or "All the Pretty Little Horses."

Children who enter the classroom carrying personal stress need strategies of adaptation. Songs comfort and massage the heart. Music is part of our ingrained ritual; it helps build community and character. Once basic needs have been nurtured and stimulated through music, children are open to tackle more cognitive work.

Who's Absent? Integration of Math and Reading

"So, who do you notice is absent today?" I ask. The children's eyes scan the faces of their friends sitting on the oval as several of them shout out in unison, "Areyel's absent!"

"Good noticing!"

A few seconds later I hear, "Munira's missing!" Most of the children answer this question by observing, but I see a few peeking over at the "Who's Absent?" chart to help guide their response. Using this opportunity to integrate letter-sound associations, I ask, "How did you know Areyel and Munira are absent? Tyrus, can you find their name cards on the 'Who's Absent?' chart? What letter does *Areyel* begin with?"

"*A*," they respond.

"And what sound does *A* make?"

"*Aaaay.*"

Then I ask, "What letter does *Munira* begin with?" and "What sound does *M* make?" (Later in the year, we switch to reading only last names on the attendance board.)

Noticing who is missing, as opposed to who is present, communicates a strong message of the importance of community. Our missing friends are significant members of our classroom. Time and again, when a child returns to school after being absent for several days, it is a classroom celebration; she is once again part of our community. A child walks through the door after an absence, and her classmates exclaim, "Munira's back, Mrs. Kempton!" Typically, hugs follow. I always reinforce this reunion, saying things like "We're glad you're back, Munira. We missed you, sweetheart."

Each morning, as the children notice which friends are missing, I keep track of the names they announce with my fingers in the air. "Who else is absent?" They all give a blank stare. "I know it's a boy, and his name begins with a *hu* sound."

"Halvin!" they unanimously respond.

"Great job! So that makes how many children absent?"

"Three!" they shout.

"When everyone is here, how many children are in our class?"

"Twenty-four," the kids exclaim.

"Let's snap back three times." The children and I simultaneously snap our fingers and count backward as I point to the number line taped across the lower section of our oval area: "Twenty-three, twenty-two, twenty-one. Good job! Who's the counter this week? Come on, Olivia, would you count the children? Remember, start with yourself."

She begins by counting her own head and continues around the oval while the rest of the class and I count along. When Olivia gets to the twenty-first person, I say, "And if Areyel were here, that would be twenty-two." All the children repeat the number. "And if Munira were here, that would be twenty-three. And if Halvin were here, that would be twenty-four!" Using my fingers to count on, the children add their missing friends to those who are present.

"So how many children are absent today?"

"Three!" they all respond confidently.

"Good job, everyone. Scoot over to the message board."

What We Can Learn

Contextual opportunities promote learning much better than isolated tasks. Attendance, something mundane that we all must do as teachers, engages children when it becomes their job to critically evaluate who is missing. The routine weaves together basic numeration skills—one-to-one correspondence, counting on (a precursor to addition), counting backward (a precursor to subtraction)—and emphasizes the importance of observation, critical thinking, and letter-sound association. But most important is the message: every community member counts.

When children are comfortable with this format of taking attendance, I can integrate addition problems effortlessly. Counting the number of girls and the number of boys present and putting an oval around the two numbers can introduce the concept of sets and union. The process of snapping back described earlier can be applied to the girls' and boys' attendance. For example, I might say, "How many boys do we have, if all of them are here?" or "If Halvin is the only boy absent, how many boys do we have? This is really tricky. We're not going to count heads." Many children can process this question instantly and respond with "Eleven!" I always refer to the number line (taped at eye level) as we figure this out, giving all children the support they need.

Early in the school year, the counter counts the boys and girls separately, confirming the thinking, and then counts everyone together. I record the union on laminated paper with a transparency marker, by putting an oval around the two numbers. Later on, the designated counter records the numbers and the union, while others read the equation (see Figure 3–3).

Several months later, I introduce the plus and equals signs. The counter's job becomes more complicated at this point; he is responsible for writing an addition equation, contextually reinforcing the formation of numerals and the meaning behind abstract symbols. The counter reads the equation with help from classmates. It's fun to add variety to the attendance rituals; for example, I can include subtraction equations near the end of the year.

Coins: Integrating Math

As children sit facing the dry-erase board that we call our message board, my finger tracks each word as we collectively read the date: Monday, December 12, 2006. Real coins, with magnetic strips adhered to their backs, cling to the whiteboard and

FIGURE 3–3 *Attendance sheet demonstrating union*

correspond with the date. Friday the 9th was our previous day in school, so one nickel and four pennies are stuck to the board.

"If today is December 12th, how much money should be up here?"

"Twelve cents," they all say.

"Good job. Let's count. What's this coin?"

"A nickel."

"And how much is it worth?"

"Five!" they say, showing me all five fingers.

"Let's count the long way." All of us whisper as I tap and count the nickel five times, and then we count on loudly as I continue to point to the four pennies. "Six, seven, eight, nine," we say forcefully. "But we need twelve cents. Friday was the 9th, Saturday was the 10th, Sunday was the 11th, and today is the 12th."

As I continue to count, my fingers keep track of the additional days. "How much more money do we need?"

"Three more pennies!" the students respond. I add three pennies to the board, making twelve cents altogether. "Does anyone see something we can do?" I ask.

"Trade them in . . . exchange!" several kids shout in unison.

"Yeah! But what are we going to exchange?"

"The pennies!"

"How many pennies?"

"Five!" they shout.

"For what?" I ask. This flurry of banter continues until they conclude that five pennies equal one nickel.

Two nickels and two pennies now rest on the board. "This is really tricky . . . does anyone see something else we could do?"

Several children respond, "Trade them in for a dime!"

"How many nickels am I going to trade in?" I ask.

"Two!" they respond.

Now one dime rests alongside two pennies. "Who can help me write a 'ten plus' problem?" I query. The concept of "ten plus" is fundamental in understanding place value and the worth of teen numbers.

Francisco shares his thinking: "Put a ten under the dime and two under the pennies."

"Good job, Francisco. And how do you show altogether?"

"Put an oval around it!" I record ten and a union of two equals twelve under the corresponding coins. "So twelve is made up of ten [I display all ten of my fingers to the children on my left] and two [I display just two fingers to the children on my right]." We whisper quietly, "One, two, three, four, . . . eight, nine, ten," as I tap the value of the dime and then count on loudly, "eleven, twelve!" as I point to the pennies. (See Figure 6–8 for a photo of our message board with the date and coins on it.)

"Let's count the fast way!" I say as I reach for my abacus. The first row is made of five purple and five green beads, and the second row contains five yellow and five orange. The children know that each color represents five (or one nickel), and each row is ten (two nickels or one dime). When one row is pushed over, they know it retains a constant value of ten (one dime). If you don't have access to an abacus, snapping your fingers and then counting on from the number can be quite effective as well.

What We Can Learn

Identifying coins, knowing their value, recognizing numerals, and understanding the concept of addition are all kindergarten math expectations. Connecting these skills with the date is a natural opportunity for integration. I begin the year as I do with the attendance ritual, demonstrating the union of two groups with an oval. Midway through the year I introduce the plus and equals signs.

I introduce the use of coins gradually, starting with the penny and emphasizing its value while reinforcing counting skills, one-to-one correspondence, and numeral recognition. The dime comes during the second month of school, reinforcing recognition of the teen numbers, the concept of "ten plus" numerals, and the introduction of place value. I introduce the nickel in the third month, but I typically wait until January to bring in the quarter, though the students have seen it and heard me refer to its value prior to that time.

The benefit of attaching coin values to dates is repetition; we're spiraling back on skills and broadening understanding of both numeration and coin value. As the year progresses, coins and number sentences can increase in complexity, depending on the strengths of the children. For example, day twenty-eight can be represented with two dimes plus eight pennies or one quarter plus three pennies.

■ Where to Start

- On your drive to or from school, take one small piece of instruction in your day and think about how it fits with something else you have discussed or will introduce. Devise a way to make this connection explicit to children.
- Slow down to reflect on and question how you can expand a particular piece of information into other subject areas. Talk to a colleague over lunch; others may have seen a relationship you missed. (Remember, learning can still be connected the following day, week, or month.)
- Observe body language; look for animated expressions. Listen to children's communication, words expressing "Why?" "What if . . . ?" "Wow!" or "That's just like . . ."
- When you introduce something new (e.g., a skill, a concept, literature), look for ways to connect it to other things going on in the classroom.

The Power of Talk

Reading and writing float on a sea of talk.

—James Britton

4

Talk is the root of literacy. To make their way in the world, children need not only knowledge but the ability to articulate that knowledge—not just to *know* but to *show*. Language is the way we show what we know, the way we make learning visible. A thousand things I do in the classroom every day aim to promote thoughtful talk, to help children open up and take risks with language.

Over time I've developed strategies for modeling and eliciting quality talk—and, just as important, quality *listening*—in each of the three domains. In the following story about Tyrus, you can see our interaction moving from one domain to the other. And you can see that before talk, even before listening, comes the first skill a teacher needs: observing.

■ Whoa, What's That Crocodile Doing?

Tyrus sat wide-eyed in the middle of the oval one early September morning, staring at an illustration of a mother crocodile with her jaws slightly open.

I strolled over and crouched down beside him. "Tyrus, what do you notice?"

"The babies are in the mouth," he said in an awestruck voice.

"Yes, they are. Are you wondering—are you wanting to know—*why* the baby crocodiles are in the mother crocodile's mouth?"

Tyrus nodded silently.

"Can you say that? Can you say, 'I wonder why the baby crocodiles . . .'?"

"I wonder why the baby crocodiles are in the mother's mouth."

"Great question, Tyrus! What do you think the answer might be?"

Tyrus shrugged.

"Well, do you think the mommy wants to *eat* her babies?"

He immediately shook his head no.

"Hmm. If the mommy didn't want to eat her babies, then *why* might she put them in her mouth?"

Tyrus didn't know, and at this point, the answer didn't really matter. We were working in the cognitive domain, where my goal is simply to stimulate thinking. In the cognitive domain, process matters more than product; learning to articulate a question takes precedence over finding the answer. Tyrus was learning to use the simple words *I wonder* when he bumped into something he couldn't figure out for himself.

The next day, when I saw Tyrus looking at the crocodile picture in the *Zoobooks* magazine again, I reminded him about our question and then started shifting our inquiry to the creative domain, where new learning happens.

"You were wondering why the mommy crocodile was carrying her babies in her mouth, remember?" I said. "Do you know where we might find the answer to that question?"

Tyrus pointed to the caption to the right of the illustration. "Yes, Tyrus, you're so smart! That writing near the picture is called a *caption*." I had him repeat the new word, then I explained it. "Usually a caption tells you what's going on in a picture. So let's read this caption. It says that mommy crocodiles *protect* their babies by carrying them around in their mouths. That's the safest place for the babies. Isn't that cool?"

I could almost see the wheels of discovery turning in Tyrus' mind as a proud smile spread across his face. "Is this new learning for you, Tyrus—something you didn't know before?" He nodded. "Wow! That's great! Can you say, 'I discovered . . . '?"

"I discovered that mommy crocodiles protect their babies by carrying them in their mouths."

Tyrus had entered the creative domain when he solved the mystery of the baby crocodiles. Now I wanted to reinforce the learning by adding the third domain, the emotional. Of course a teacher can't—and wouldn't want to—do this with every student's question every day. But in this case the opportunity and the time were there, and I thought that looking through one more kind of lens would help Tyrus anchor his new vocabulary. So I asked him more questions.

"What if *you* were a baby crocodile? Can you imagine wiggling around beside your brothers and sisters inside your mommy's mouth? How do you think you might feel in there, looking out at the world?"

"Scared?" Tyrus ventured tentatively. I'd expected this response because children view most situations literally: a baby's soft skin plus a mother crocodile's sharp teeth equal, in a child's mind, fear.

"Yeah, I can see how you might be scared because of all those sharp teeth! Hmm. Remember what we read in the caption? Mommy crocodiles *protect* their babies by holding them in their mouths. If your mommy was protecting you from all the other animals that might hurt you, *then* how would you feel?"

"Safe!"

"Yes! The mouth is the very safest place you could be. So you would feel . . ."

"Protected!" (This is a word my students know because it comes up often in class, for instance, when our box turtle pulls her head inside her shell.)

Although my conversation with Tyrus did not involve reading or writing, it represented a crucial step in literacy: making sense of pictures and expressing thinking. Too often, teachers minimize the importance of observing and speaking, which are huge motivators for children—if someone is there to listen. Talk engages children with the learning process, and the quality of talk deepens when you support children in expressing themselves. Because we are teaching emergent writers and readers, our literacy block must rest on a solid foundation of oral language experiences, emphasizing the reciprocity of talk, writing, and reading.

■ Why Talk?

The context of talk is generated when I ask, "Who's got something to share? What did you discover? Tell me more." Promoting thoughtful, reflective talk requires creating an environment where children feel safe, where they know their feelings and thoughts will be validated. When children feel valued as important contributing members of the community, they are more willing to take risks with language; taking those risks builds confidence and self-esteem.

Here's a quick outline of the reasons that nurturing and developing discourse are so important in kindergarten. It's helpful to have this list at your fingertips when administrators walk into your classroom and see you and the children talking. You can then eloquently state why you value this important time.

- Talk is the underlying thread of literacy.
- Talk enriches experience and expands language across the curriculum.
- Talk facilitates retention and enhances comprehension.
- Talk motivates and engages children in their learning.
- Talk develops oral language, creates new schema, and clarifies meaning.
- Talk fosters risk taking in language.
- Talk strengthens community.

- Talk shows comprehension.
- Talk empowers a child.

Because talk expands opportunities in all subject areas, I work to cultivate it everywhere: in community, sharing, literacy, movement, math, science, and play. "Research shows that children learn better by hearing multiple representations of knowledge, and by exposure to the thinking processes of co-learners. Classroom dialogue secures memory and adds depth and meaning to the educational experience. Students need to speak fluently before they can be expected to read fluently" (Pitcairn 2006, 26).

Talk motivates children to engage actively in the learning process. When teachers listen to children and ask questions to elicit talk, oral language develops, new schema is created, and meaning is clarified, laying a foundation for critical thinking. The quality of talk deepens when we give children the time and support to express themselves. Talk expands children's world, putting wonder and discovery at the forefront of their learning.

How children express themselves is, of course, the way teachers know they are learning. To master self-expression, children need large uninterrupted periods of time to converse, ask questions, and play with language. Our classroom schedule offers many safe, predictable chances to talk: in oval share; after writing, reading, or math; during choice time; and at the end of the day. Children know they're welcome to use those times to talk about their experiences or the things they wonder about.

It's important to design both your schedule and your room to encourage thoughtful talk. With young children, a large open space in the form of a circle or oval, defined by the placement of a rug or of tape on the floor, is a good place to start. Next, show children good community behaviors: sitting flat on their bottoms (so they don't obstruct their neighbor) with legs crossed and hands to themselves and staying quiet while others are speaking. Children feel safe to share when it's quiet and they can see their friends' attentive faces around the circle, rather than the backs they'd see if everyone sat in rows.

When I model quality talk, I listen with interest to what is being shared. Children are astute and immediately read my level of engagement. I choose my own shares selectively: the first snowfall of the year and how peaceful it looks, or the discovery of a worm retracting instantly when a flashlight illuminates its hole. Only through repeated modeling do children come to understand what's expected in the tone and content of talk. Modeling listening is even more important than modeling talk; the minute the talk becomes my agenda, children shut down. Once children are talking, keeping things going becomes a dance of listening, asking questions, drawing out information, and restating ideas. I listen for opportunities to deepen literary experience, expand vocabulary, and weave together previous learning. Questioning and determining importance become key processes in shaping a dialogue.

Everything I do aims to help children's voices grow stronger throughout the year in different contexts of learning. I informally evaluate this accomplishment by noticing how often a child talks, how he retains and expands language, and whether he can articulate thoughts or discoveries without prompting.

Characteristics of Quality Talk

At first, any talk is good talk. You listen, then gradually encourage children to expand their thinking and talking. You do this by asking questions, paraphrasing what you hear, and providing specific language when necessary. You know you're hearing quality talk when your support leads children to say more than you, or they, thought possible. Through quality talk, teachers and children

- balance personal shares with nonfiction discoveries, providing different contexts in which to expand language
- demonstrate investment by genuinely listening
- showcase a point to the talk, which could be an emotional experience or a new discovery
- choose subjects that interest most of the group (animals, their families, emotional experiences)
- trigger dialogue by asking interesting, relevant questions
- choose topics that lend themselves to vocabulary development, schema development, and integrated learning

■ Why Listen?

The only route to great talk is great listening. As a child speaks, I pay close attention, modeling listening in the way I stay quiet and then ask questions, draw out thoughts, and support and develop language. (Meanwhile, of course, I'm redirecting inappropriate behavior from others.) Establishing and maintaining respect is an essential element in building a community of listeners and learners. When we establish our oval time at the beginning of the year, I explain that this is a special part of our day when we share important things going on in our lives, questions we have, and discoveries we have made.

"It's important that when someone shares, we are respectful of him or her," I tell the children. "We learn so much from our friends. Respect can be shown in different ways. In our classroom, we show respect by sitting flat on our bottoms, on the edge of the tape so I can see everyone's face, legs crossed, hands in our laps, voices off, and eyes on the person who is sharing. If any of this is uncomfortable to you, please let me know (e.g., giving someone eye contact)." By continually enforcing these listening behaviors, I build a culture of respect that strongly communicates an essential message: we are all teachers and learners.

When listening to a child, simply notice any interesting or unusual bit of information and begin asking questions about it. As you slowly pull out threads of experience, you help the child piece thoughts together into a cohesive story. Paraphrasing what a child communicates helps expand vocabulary and self-expression not just for that child but for others who are listening as well.

Listening to a child's innermost thoughts is the highest form of respect a teacher can give. As Gail Sher beautifully stated in *One Continuous Mistake*, "A story cradles the psyche. Listening becomes a form of embrace" (1999, 131). Having children listen and ask questions of one another provides tremendous learning opportunities for all. Children's firsthand or vicarious experiences become richer when they express them verbally. We all refer to these conversations and discoveries through the days and weeks and build on them throughout the year. The experiences we remember are the rich stories remaining in our psyche.

Characteristics of Quality Listening

Listening is an integral piece of great talk. You know listening is working when teachers and children

- suspend personal agendas
- use engaging eye contact
- refrain from talking while others are sharing
- paraphrase and reflect comprehension
- ask relevant questions
- recognize everyone as a member of the classroom community

■ The Many Contexts of Talk

As talk happens throughout the day, the context determines the content. A context, such as play, can be used to focus on various content areas. For example, in outdoor play, the content of literature and math appears in the form of jumping rope and reciting nursery rhymes and math chants. And sometimes, in an almost magical way, the playground can turn out to be a child's best classroom.

Abdili's First Jump

Abdili (*AHB-doo-lie*) entered my room at the beginning of the year with little to no affect; it seemed he didn't know what a smile was. Having arrived only recently from Somalia, he had limited experience with our language.

One morning on the playground, loud rhyming chants and the slapping of ropes drew Abdili toward an experienced group of jumpers for the first time. Gingerly, I went through the basic steps, as I do with all children new to jumping rope. Through actions and words, I demonstrated how to stand in the middle of the jump rope, which is marked with a red line. "When I say, 'Jump!' I want you to blast up to the moon." The rope going over their heads scares many children because they think it will hit them. Most can progress quickly to doing consecutive jumps, but usually it takes days of practice before they can add an extra bounce to the rhythm. Abdili, however, caught on fast. Within minutes he was adding an extra bounce as a big grin widened across his face.

I gave him a huge hug, congratulating him on being such a great jumper, as he beamed and got right back into line to jump some more. The children and I began chanting, "One, two, buckle my shoe, three, four, shut the door." Thus began a pattern that continued for weeks: Abdili kept jumping happily but remained silent, listening attentively to the rhymes and internalizing their structures. Then one day he boldly began to recite with the group, giggling with confidence. The influence of his jump rope success didn't end there: during reading workshop, Abdili frequently chose jump rope rhymes as the texts he wanted to read.

What We Can Learn

Knowing the structure of language and how it works is critical in the emerging stages of reading. The playground is the perfect place to integrate the content of literature and math and to play with language. Because children need familiarity with sounds, they benefit from continually hearing language structures repeated. I begin by introducing jumping rhymes such as "Teddy Bear, Teddy Bear," "Cinderella Dressed in Yellow," and "Bubblegum, Bubblegum in a Dish." When children have internalized these language structures, they confidently choose the texts from our classroom bins and "read" the rhymes on their own, just as Abdili did.

Experiencing rhythm and identifying patterns directly affect reading fluency. Once these structures are well known, children can predict expected patterns in print. "Early readers must first hear abundant spoken language. They must playfully interact with language through rhyming and other word play before they are ready to decode sounds and sound sequences. Adequate oral language experience is prerequisite to, and highly predictive of, reading success" (Pitcairn 2006, 26).

Once rhymes are internalized, it's fun to play with language and adapt them. Here's an example of an adaptation the children and I made one morning while jumping rope: "Cinderella, dressed in black, went downstairs and had a snack. How many snacks did she have?" With right arm and palm extended, the children and I made a scooping motion in the air to eye level as we said the word *black*. We took our left arm (palm extended, scooping upward) to the same level as the right palm as we said the word *snack*. Because the words rhymed, we kept our palms level. To contrast a word that didn't rhyme, we scooped our right hand, once again, to eye level with *black*. Then we said the word *soup*, which obviously doesn't rhyme, and stopped at chest level with our left palm, demonstrating a mismatch in rhyme.

Numerous math skills can be chanted as well. "Skip count, skip count, count by twos . . ." (or by ones, fives, tens, etc.). Whenever we finish a counting rhyme, I ask the children how to represent the numeral. I draw it in the palm of my hand with my pointer finger and then encourage them to draw in the air as well, reinforcing numeral formation and identification.

Every second of the day is a teachable moment. For Abdili, a seemingly small thing like jumping rope had a major impact. This new physical activity bolstered his self-esteem, taught him about rhythm and language structure, and helped prepare him for reading. As the community supported Abdili, he began not just reciting but inventing his own rhymes. His playground prowess moved him a long way down the road in building esteem and self-confidence.

■ The Big Picture of Integration

The following four stories correlate through common threads: safety, appropriate responses to threat, and new vocabulary like *threatened* and *protected*. The first story begins in the contexts of sharing, community, and literacy as we discuss a classroom social issue on the oval. The second story involves integrating content—new emotional vocabulary, science, and literature—into the context of movement, giving depth and breadth to a read-aloud. In the third story, movement again elicits vocabulary and supports language retention. The fourth story demonstrates the importance of purpose in writing—and, of course, the power of talk.

The Power in "Using Your Words"

Toneeshia was having difficulty adjusting to our classroom community. Never having been in school before, she lacked the social and emotional skills other children had acquired from preschool experience. Her classmates complained about her crude language and verbal threats. After several days of repeated complaints, Toneeshia was removed from the classroom and spent the remaining part of the day detained in in-school suspension.

The following morning she returned to class. I welcomed her with a hug and openly discussed her behavior with the class on the oval. Telling others that she was going to "beat them up" was not OK talk, I told the group. "Frightening others doesn't make us feel safe. School is a place for learning, and in order to learn, we need to feel safe.

"This is really important for all of you to understand. Toneeshia is not a bad girl. She is kind and sweet, and I love her dearly. Her behavior was not a good choice. It's never OK to hurt anyone in any way. This is one of our most important school rules. Can you all do your best thinking and learning if you're worrying about getting beat up?"

"No!" they all responded.

"Alicia, would you 'use your words' with Toneeshia, and let her know how you feel about what she said to you?"

Through watching my repeated modeling and observing others, Alicia had grown skilled at this ritual. She sat in front of Toneeshia, looked her in the eye, and said, "Toneeshia, I don't like you saying mean words to me and telling me you're going beat up my mother. That makes me feel sad and mad."

"Alicia, does it also make you feel scared?" I asked. She nodded. "Well, you need to tell Toneeshia that as well."

"That makes me feel scared when you say mean things and tell me you're going to beat up my mother."

"Good job, sweetheart. And what do you want from Toneeshia?"

"I don't want you saying mean words to me or telling me you're going to beat up my mother."

Tenderly I said, "Toneeshia, what did you hear Alicia say to you?"

"She don't want me to say mean things to her."

"That's right. She doesn't want you to say mean things to her, and . . . what about her mother?"

"She don't want me beating up her mother."

"That's really close, Toneeshia. She doesn't want you *saying* you're going to beat up her mother. Would you please tell Alicia you're not going to beat her up and you're not going to talk about beating up her mother?"

With my support, Toneeshia accurately reiterated to Alicia what I'd asked. "Good job, sweetheart. Would you please tell the rest of your friends this as well?"

Again, with support, she repeated to the class, "I won't tell you I'm going to beat you up, or your mother, anymore."

"Thank you, sweetheart. That really helps your friends feel safe. We can do a much better job of thinking and learning now."

Protected Like a Snail

We continued our talk on the oval. "So how does it feel when you don't feel safe?" I asked.

Several children responded "sad" and "scared."

"Remember the word Auriyah used the other day to describe how you might feel if someone was doing mean things to you?" It was a great word, *threatened*, and this seemed like an ideal opportunity to reinforce that new emotional vocabulary.

We had been working on visualization as a comprehension strategy, noticing how great writers use words to paint a picture for their readers. I carried this thread of new vocabulary through the literature we were reading. In *The Snail's Spell*, by Joanne Ryder (1982), a snail feels threatened and quickly retracts its feelers, and its eyeballs slide down, down, back into its body. Of course, I provided the opportunity for the children to reenact this process in the middle of the oval.

To the beat of a drum, the children shrank themselves to "inch size" as they slowly stretched their bodies along the imagined damp, brown ground. As they safely inched along, their feelers stretched upward and the eyeballs glided up to the tips. The snails searched eagerly for food. Sure enough, around the bend a green lettuce leaf awaited! With tongues outstretched, they used rows and rows of teeth to scrape the delicious greenery. Then a cat wandered into the garden, taking them by surprise. Within seconds, all my little snails felt threatened, instantly retracting their eyeballs and feelers and pulling their soft bodies back inside their hard shells.

As the children reenacted this experience, my language echoed their actions: "You no longer feel safe and secure. You feel *threatened*. Quickly! Pull your feelers back, and let your eyeballs glide back down into your body. Pull yourself back into your hard shell so you feel safe. Now you are *protected*."

It Exsprouted!

A week later during writing workshop, I was conferring with Michael when he began to tell me a story. At first he didn't have the language to describe what had happened, so he said just this: "Loud cars . . . windows broke . . . a whole bunch!" I inferred it was probably a drive-by shooting and didn't want to emphasize the shooting part. "What were the windows made of?" I asked. No response. I tapped on the glass prism sitting nearby, eliciting the word *glass* from him.

"So the window glass broke? Show me what happened." He made tight fists with both hands and burst them quickly apart, flinging his arms left and right. "Wow!" I said. "What word could you use to describe what the glass did?"

"Ex-*sprouted!*" Michael said enthusiastically.

We had recently sprouted pumpkin seeds in a root garden and taped a plastic bag with these seeds inside to our classroom window so we could observe what usually happens underground. We'd discussed how a pumpkin seed pop opens—sprout! "Michael, what you did with your hands is so great! The word you're showing is *exploded*."

With my support, he recorded in his daybook, "THE WNDO GLAS XPLOD!" (*The window glass exploded!*).

Later, as he sat in the author's chair relating his experience, I asked, "How did you feel, Michael, as the glass exploded?"

"Scared!" he said.

"Yeah, I'm sure you did. Remember that rich word we used to describe feeling not safe, not protected?"

Michael and several others immediately responded, "Threatened!"

"Yes. As the glass exploded, you felt threatened."

Write for a Reason

Not long afterward, we had another chance to revisit the meaning of our new vocabulary and demonstrate various purposes for writing. After singing "May All Children," a beautiful song written in memory of 9/11, I explained to the children, "We write for a reason. It's so we don't forget our happiest or saddest memories or important things in our lives. The person who wrote this song didn't want a horrible event like this ever to happen again. Ken Guilmartin wrote it so we wouldn't forget. The song is for children, so little ones can grow up in a world where they feel safe and protected, not threatened."

Malicah astutely interjected, "So they can be mommies and daddies."

"Yes."

The children listened attentively to this explanation. We were ready to move on with our morning when Auriyah, who had clearly been thinking it all over, blurted out her question: "Why didn't those people driving the planes watch where they were going?"

Wow—Auriyah obviously didn't understand that the events of 9/11 were deliberate, even though we had previously discussed this at great length. Her question opened up a critical opportunity for me to clarify for everyone, once again, what I had taken for granted. Further discussion and more writing by various children surfaced after this episode.

■ What We Can Learn

I draw out children's thinking so that it becomes visible. The primary way to accomplish this is through talk. Talk provides opportunities for children to clarify meaning, ask questions, play with language, and synthesize information.

Our community became unstable when a new member disrespected social boundaries. Toneeshia's behavior required attention in everyone's presence, so that children could feel safe and focused while learning. Alicia's modeling of how to stand up to Toneeshia by using her words was powerful communication. Her example reinforced for everyone that specific language helps communicate feelings and leads to desirable outcomes.

I deliberately address behavioral issues such as these with the whole class, so there is no mystery regarding a child's conduct. Talk in the context of community reinforces school and classroom boundaries and strengthens our communal ties. Providing safe environments for communication and setting consistent boundaries both help create communities built on trust, understanding, and compassion.

These behavioral expectations are repeatedly conveyed in my classroom and the rest of the school. It's important to make the distinction between a child and that child's behavior. The child is not bad; rather, she made poor choices. Teachers and administrators in our school use this language regularly, and it has helped tremendously with discipline issues.

Similarly, children need consistent language to communicate feelings accurately so that they are understood by friends and teachers. Exact language is critical in having others hear our voice. If language does not accurately depict emotions, we can't appreciate and support a child's experience. I teach children a concise format to use when someone is bothering them. I repeatedly model and support this language in the classroom throughout the year:

- "I don't like it when . . . (you are pushing me in line)." Key: Be specific about the behavior.
- "I feel (mad or sad) when . . . (you push me in line)." Key: Introduce emotional vocabulary.
- "I want you to . . . (stop pushing me in line)." Key: Specify a desired outcome.

To start, children need support in using this structure and describing the specific behavior of another child. As the first child communicates each step, it's important that the other child actively listens and then repeats back the words she's heard. Often, the listening child needs to hear the communication repeated, or broken down into smaller chunks, before she can echo the first child's words. This process does take time initially, but the gains far outweigh the time spent in the end.

Active listening is necessary because so many young children are truly unaware of their behavior. They didn't realize they were pushing their friends; they were just in a hurry to get in line. People who aren't aware of their actions can't change their behavior. Supporting children in using specific language helps them to become confident, self-directed learners.

Talking about feelings gives children permission to share within the emotional domain, and later to return to this domain in their writing, reading, and future learning. So, for example, by listening carefully and supporting Alicia in clearly articulating her experience to Toneeshia, I honored both her feelings and her ability to take action. Respect, empathy, community, and boundaries were all strengthened as a result.

As children feel safer in the classroom, risk taking with language expands. Michael's and Auriyah's stories are great examples of making thinking visible so I could clarify their thoughts. Both of them felt safe enough to try new language and new inquiries. Michael's share demonstrated the use of movement as a tool to draw out and facilitate language development. Once he attempted to express the word he was searching for, I clarified and used his great hand movements to help the class retain language and expand vocabulary schema. "Everyone, show me *exploded*." The children clutched their fists together into a ball and burst them apart, while adding a combustive sound.

Without opportunities for talk, the expansion of language and learning in all these scenarios would never have happened. Learning would have been severely curtailed.

◼ Where to Start

- Reflect on your day and the opportunities to weave talk into various contexts.
- Set aside time in your schedule to begin modeling a specific kind of talk (math, science, emotional) for the children.
- Encourage students to join you in dialogue.
- Provide children with language structures and specific language you want them to use. Have them repeat these structures to provide a framework for their talk, for example, "I discovered …" or "I felt …"
- Ask sensory questions (e.g., "What did it look, taste, feel, sound, smell like?") to help elicit language.
- Actively listen and then paraphrase and ask questions to clarify ideas.
- Provide language for a child when he doesn't have words to express himself. Try other avenues, such as movement or drawing, to elicit talk. "Ah, well you call that a _____. Can you say _____? So, you were _____ and you saw a _____. Tell me more."
- Listen for opportunities to make a child's learning and thinking visible so all can benefit. Listen attentively for interesting, unusual bits of information a child might share, and begin asking questions, slowly pulling out threads of a story or experience.

- Look for nonverbalized learning (a drawing, block construction, or writing sample), and support a child in making her learning known. For example, if a child has constructed a pattern that moves out in a circle, you can draw out the language to help her describe what she's built or drawn.

Play

The most effective kind of education is that a child should play amongst lovely things.

—Plato

5

In the mornings, the oval on our classroom floor is the place for sharing, reading, and movement. In the afternoons it's for lots of other things—group work, math manipulatives, and one of my favorites, big blocks. But in my first weeks of teaching at Harrington, the center of the oval sat empty in the afternoons. The big blocks, hollow wooden squares (about one foot long) and rectangles (about two feet long), stayed like silent soldiers in neat ranks against the walls.

Knowing that the children hadn't played with such large shapes before, I tried introducing the big blocks gradually, talking about shapes and sizes and modeling how to put together some rudimentary constructions. Few children took my lead. Now and then during choice time (when students can play where they please), a child would pull out a few of the big blocks, only to put them back moments later and go do something else.

Play is the work of children, the most natural thing they do. Just as with any component of learning, however, making the most of a particular kind of play can require direction and support—from a teacher or sometimes from other children. It takes only one interested, confident child to shift the energy, and I knew just the girl to do it: Chantel. Bubbly, verbal, and independent, she was a born enthusiast; whatever she was doing always looked to the other kids like the most fun *ever*.

"Chantel," I called one day as she headed across the room from the dramatic play area. She didn't appear to be involved in anything, so it seemed like a good time to try sparking some class interest in these cool blocks. "Why don't you come over to the big blocks and try building something?" Somewhat reluctantly, she started pulling small wooden squares and rectangles into the open space. Large rectangles soon followed. Within minutes she was hauling blocks by the armload and shouting her enthusiasm across the room. Other children stopped to stare at the oval, usually so empty and now a crazy jumble of shapes and sizes.

At my suggestion, Chantel began combining two large rectangles to make a bench for sitting. Next came two squares spaced apart, with a long slat board resting on top: a simple table. By this time, DaMarqus (*Da-MAR-kis*), RahShay, Caesauna (*KAY-shah-na*), Alexis, Michael, Jesse, and Yasmeen had joined her. Tremendous dialogue, laughter, and enthusiasm followed as the building crew carted nearly every block in the room into the center of the oval.

"Hey!" Chantel shouted. "Let's build a *giant* table!" Her enthusiasm spread like wildfire. All the children were engaged, thrilled with the novelty of building on a grand scale. Chantel gave directions on what to put where, and her friends eagerly complied. Before long they had supersized the original small, narrow construction by extending four rows of twelve-inch squares on either side and layering more four-foot slats across the top. And there it was: the giant table Chantel had envisioned. Soon benches, each made from two large rectangles, adorned all four sides.

"Gosh, this is incredible," I said, coming over to admire the project. "Look at what you guys built!" Broad grins stretched across their faces. "So . . . what kind of a table is this?" They met my enthusiasm with shrugs and blank stares. They'd been building for the fun of building; who cared about the table's purpose? I walked away to let the question linger.

Apparently, however, my question had planted a seed. When I looked over a few minutes later, I saw an amazing sight: All eight children were sitting at their new table, writing with colored pencils on sheets of white paper. In all my years of teaching, this was the first time a group of children had created a table specifically designated for writing. It was amazing to witness this collective enthusiasm swell and direct itself. Some of my most squirmy children were focused and engaged, writing purposefully with the colored pencils. In the next few weeks, the group created versions of this large-scale construction over and over again, drawing others into the writing table project.

■ Much More than Fun

For the children, the meaning of this building experience probably consisted of a single word: *fun*. For me, it was so much more. Play forms a natural context for integrating all sorts of concepts and skills into children's learning. And when the play involves creating life-size environments—tables, houses, forts, anything the kids can actually play in—the benefits stack up fast (see Figure 5–1).

FIGURE 5–1 *Children engage in gross motor problem solving with big blocks.*

As they work with various sizes of large, hollow blocks, children are kinesthetically exploring the relationships between size, shape, area, and volume, all important concepts in both science and math. According to the National Association for the Education of Young Children (NAEYC), "When a child builds a structure or represents the world symbolically with houses, bridges, ramps, and tunnels, he is dealing with geographical concepts as well as with scientific concepts of space, distance, direction, grids, patterns, and mapping." (1974, 25). If their tabletop falls, or the roof of their fort repeatedly crashes to the floor, children quickly realize why they need to know principles of symmetry and balance (see Figure 5–2).

In building the giant table, the children were encountering not just mathematical and scientific concepts, which exist in the cognitive domain, but also concepts like team planning and cooperation, which reside firmly in the emotional domain. And of course the project offered infinite possibilities for creativity: imagining and then creating new pieces of furniture in new shapes and styles, and bringing in other materials—in the case of the writing table, paper and pencils—to make the space functional.

Nobody needs to teach a child to play, but good teachers do help move play into new areas of learning by observing, listening, asking questions, encouraging new directions, clarifying ideas, and—this one isn't always easy—relinquishing control. In my first year of teaching, the idea of letting children play freely felt overwhelming.

FIGURE 5–2 *Children build with small blocks, exploring symmetry and balance.*

So I structured everything: I assigned children to color groups and rotated them through designated activities during the course of the week, ensuring that they experienced every play area of the classroom whether it interested them or not.

All that structure began losing significance as I came to understand the five-year-old. Children this age thrive on choice and varied means of self-expression. Not all kindergartners want, or need, to explore all areas of play. Children who don't have lots of dolls or blocks at home will be drawn to those things at school, while other children's interests may lie elsewhere. I decided to try letting the children choose which play areas would keep them focused and stimulated, and my intuition was right on. I found that the key is to trust the kids and to explicitly model expectations for what play environments look and sound like.

Watching children enjoy themselves is one of the best parts of teaching kindergarten, but you're never *only* watching; you're always on the lookout for the next teachable moment. If I hadn't asked Chantel and her crew, "So what kind of a table did you build?" they probably would not have moved beyond construction to thinking about *purpose*. By encouraging them to keep their minds as well as their hands in motion, my attentiveness and my questions nudged them into the creative domain.

◼ Keeping Play Alive

Once I'd given up the idea of controlling play, choice time became one of my favorite times of the day. This is when children are free to explore, learn, and interact with other children and materials in any way they wish. All our classroom areas are available: dramatic play, art, easel, water table, workbench, big blocks, small blocks, plastic interlocking building bricks, listening center, math, science, classroom animals, and writing area. I love the children's joyful faces. I love to listen to their imaginative dialogue and watch them explore and create new structures. This is the children's time to make independent choices, learn from others, express themselves in a less structured manner, and experience joy.

But a teacher can't just sit back and let play happen. As counterintuitive as the idea may sound at first, even choice time requires constant monitoring. I've encountered the pattern often enough to recognize it quickly: For about a month, children will do wonderful things during choice time. Then suddenly they'll start acting silly or mistreating the materials, and I'll have to set boundaries. I used to get upset when this happened, until I realized that the problem wasn't them; it was me. I'd worked to build a context for play, but I needed to work harder to *sustain* that context. If the teacher is the conductor, she can't expect the kindergarten orchestra to play harmoniously without good, well-tuned instruments and lots of practice.

So when choice time starts feeling stale, I know it's time to shake things up—turn the playhouse into a store, bring out sewing materials or weaving as an option, or introduce the marble chute. New teaching always accompanies these additions. Some of the instruction, such as showing children how to use tools before allowing them to work at the workbench, is planned and scheduled (see Figure 5–3). But many more kinds of coaching happen on the spot. For example, if I see a child in the playhouse answering the telephone, I'll hand him paper and pencil and

FIGURE 5–3 *Francisco focuses on sawing as Bella hammers away.*

FIGURE 5–4 *Noehlie takes a note using a phone book.*

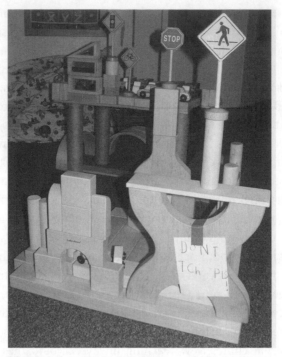

FIGURE 5–5 *Finished construction with sign in place that reads, "Don't Touch, Please!"*

FIGURE 5–6 *Haley and Adol sing lullabies to Floppy.*

encourage him to take a message. Kids see themselves as *playing* when they write this note. Play, not writing time, is the lens they're looking through (see Figure 5–4).

Integrating learning looks different depending on the play areas that children choose. Whether they're writing signs in the block area (see Figure 5–5), cooking meals in the playhouse, singing lullabies to Floppy in the rocker (see Figure 5–6), or using a ruler to measure a piece of wood at the workbench, practical application of learning is my ultimate goal.

Generating and sustaining a context for play is a long-term process that requires focused attention and continual fine-tuning. If children are being disrespectful of materials or friends, I take choice time away. I am very clear with them that it's their choice, not mine, to lose this precious time of the day, and I explain what they have done to bring this about. Children are empowered when they take responsibility for their actions and when the consequences of inappropriate behavior are consistently applied.

Like the conductor with his orchestra, I evaluate play through what I see and hear. Play that's veering off track grates on my ears like an out-of-tune violin. When I hear thoughtful dialogue coming from inside the playhouse walls or excited giggles (as opposed to silliness) from underneath big blocks, when I observe the intent focus of painters or of children confidently sawing and hammering wood, I experience the room working harmoniously, all players in tune. My class is learning by playing, and I'm free to imagine the next steps. (See Figure 5–7.)

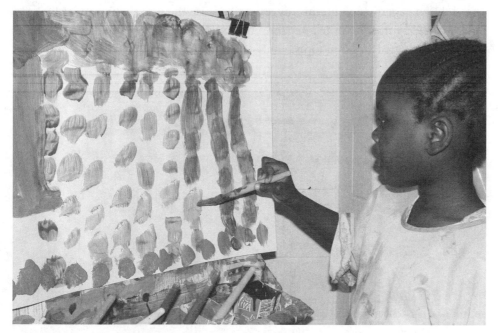

FIGURE 5–7 *Adol paints intently.*

◼ JRFS Live Here

Any subject or event can be an occasion for integrating learning and play. After we visited the Denver Zoo, the children were thrilled about reenacting this experience. Back in the classroom, they began building their own zoo with small blocks. When I placed a tub of plastic animals nearby, the kids immediately incorporated them into the construction. "Who lives here?" I asked. "Remember the signs we saw at the zoo? They were posted in front of the animals' *habitats*, their homes, so you would know the name of the animal you were looking at. How about if you guys make some signs?"

Several children quickly seized on that suggestion, writing on small notepaper with markers and using masking tape to attach each sign to the designated habitat. (Masking tape is easy for children to manipulate and doesn't leave a sticky residue.) Some of the signs included "LINS," "JRFS," "PoLRBRS," and of course "ZOO" for the front entrance. Several other children improved their habitats with water, trees, boulders, and other paper scenery they'd created in the art area. (See Figure 5–8.)

The zoo story is a simple example of how to integrate writing and meaningful play into a child's environment. After observing animals on our field trip, the children were primed to re-create what they had experienced when they returned to school. They were focused and enthused about revisiting this learning in a different area, block building, and I nudged them further by suggesting a writing component. The children eagerly took up this suggestion because the writing had a real-life purpose: to identify their favorite animals in the environment they'd built. Tackling this project empowered children to use tools—paper, scissors, markers, tape—for a con-

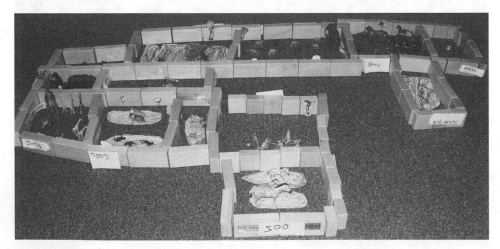

FIGURE 5–8 *Children's re-creation of the Denver Zoo*

crete reason. Providing context and purpose for play promotes integration of concepts and expands writing in meaningful ways.

◼ Pizza Shop: Integrated Learning in Dramatic Play

Several months into the school year, after children have experienced the traditional playhouse, I give them a choice to change the dramatic play area into something else: a veterinary clinic, grocery store, pizza shop, or some new environment they imagine. "I think it's time to vote on what our playhouse should become! What do you think?" This time when the class voted, the pizza shop won unanimously.

For the next few days we discussed and listed the essential props for running the shop: pizzas, delivery boxes, cups, plates, napkins, aprons, hats, money. A local pizza shop donated boxes and napkins, and we had a wooden pizza I had ordered with my classroom budget, with removable toppings, a pizza wheel for cutting, and a spatula for serving (see Figure 5–9). My daughter, Lilli, had the same wooden pizza at home, which she'd she used in her play kitchen for years; she sent it along for my students to use.

I suggested to the class that we create paper pizzas as a collage project in case someone wanted to order a large pie. During choice time, Luisa and Sheldon eagerly painted round pieces of cardboard, layering them brown for crust and red for sauce.

FIGURE 5–9 *Julia serves up a pizza and delivers a meal ticket.*

We glued on yellow and orange tissue paper strips for a cheesy texture and topped the disks with small green rectangles and red and black circles. The paper pizzas looked good enough to eat. Enthusiasm spread as the children watched the pizzas take on a lifelike form. "Hey, you should cut them, Mrs. Kempton!" Haley said.

"What a great idea, sweetheart!" I answered, seeing immediate opportunities to talk about fractions.

Next we took up signs and their purpose. "What should we name our pizza shop?" I asked. Kids responded with, "Good Pizza, Nicholas' Pizza, Delicious Pizza, Yummy Pizza . . ."

"Delicious Pizza!" the children exclaimed in unison.

"That's the name of our store?"

"Yeah!" they enthusiastically confirmed.

The class helped as Jenecia (*Jen-EE-see-ah*) and Mona wrote out a large sign naming our shop, plus other pertinent signs such as "Open" and "Closed," by stretching out the sounds associated with the letters. During choice time, Jenecia illustrated the sign "Delicious Pizza!" with scrumptious slices adorning the text. I photocopied the "Delicious Pizza!" sign and attached it to the top of the pizza boxes. Several volunteers eagerly decorated the takeout boxes with brightly colored markers. (See Figure 5–10.)

Because of the limited space in our classroom, I broke up the dramatic play area for use as the pizza kitchen, dishwashing area, and cashier's counter (see Figure 5–11). The big-block area was designated for building tables and seating, making it an integral component of the play environment. This fun and purposeful form of construction would change daily, starting with modeling possibilities for tables (small versus community tables) and demonstrating styles of chairs.

I suggested that the children begin experimenting with constructions during choice time. Tyrus took the lead and began building a medium-size table out of large rectangles and small squares, making sure both sides were balanced and using long slat boards for the table surface. I watched with enthusiasm as he effortlessly manipulated blocks to form a functional structure.

Shortly after, I was amazed to see Anayansi and Haley constructing two different styles of chairs positioned at opposite ends of the table. Two of them were low-back chairs made of squares and small rectangles, while the other two were almost thrones, with high seats and tall backs. I was surprised that the girls had remembered the basics of block construction from my introduction at the beginning of the year. I encouraged them and Tyrus to share ideas and teach others about various furniture possibilities. (See Figure 5–12.)

After finishing the table, Tyrus asked if he could build a play area.

"What for?" I wondered.

FIGURE 5–10 *Delicious Pizza! sign, pizza boxes, and homemade pizza collage*

FIGURE 5–11 *View of pizza shop showing cashier's station and eating area*

FIGURE 5–12 *Pizza table and chair constructions using big blocks*

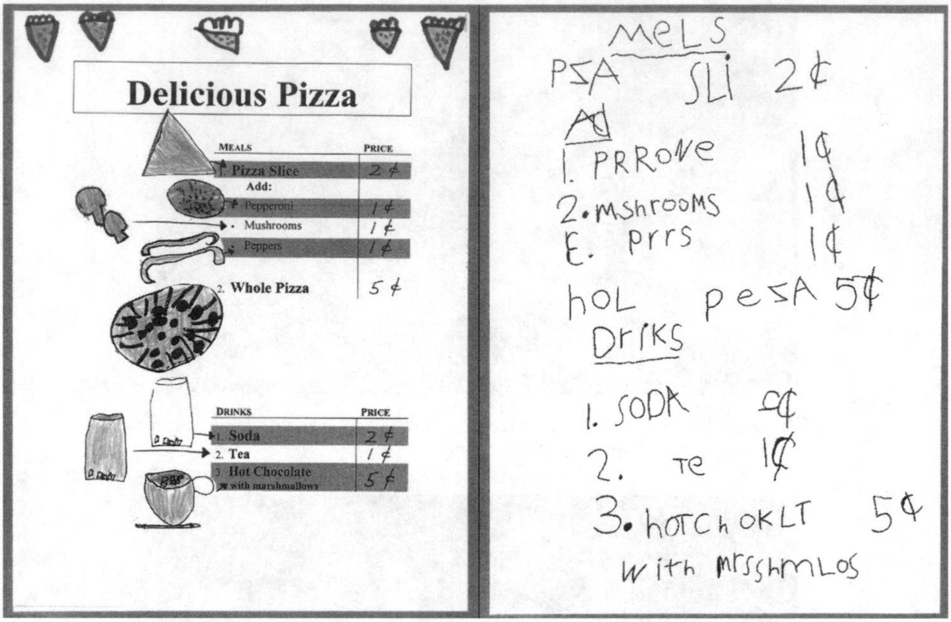

FIGURE 5–13 *Completed menu* (left) *and original writing, which was done on back of menu* (right)

"Like McDonald's!" he responded. He pulled out the wooden bridge, a prop used with big blocks, and flipped it over, creating a rocking boat.

"What an awesome idea, Tyrus!" I realized he was adding a deeper dimension to the shop, and my thoughts began following his lead. Suddenly I envisioned how other manipulatives, such as small blocks and puzzles, could be incorporated into this area. Our small-block section could be designed as the children's play space inside the pizza shop. There might be a more quiet section for reading or drawing; the possibilities were endless.

Our next task was to design a menu (see Figure 5–13), which meant supporting the children in figuring out a functional way to carry money and use manipulatives to calculate prices. We batted around dozens of other questions about operational logistics: Where would the entrance and exit be? How would the cash register function? Where would we keep pizza tickets and writing utensils? Where would customers place their orders? Where would we put the tickets so that the cook could see what toppings and drinks the customers had ordered? Where would people wait if there weren't enough tables? Would we have waitresses or waiters, busboys or hostesses? How would everything—money, pizza, toppings, plates, napkins, boxes, dress-up clothes, blocks—be returned to its designated spot efficiently when the pizza shop closed?

Answering these complex questions required teamwork, critical thinking, and problem-solving skills, but the kids saw the process simply as fun. As they devised their solutions, some of which I'd never have thought of myself, they were firing on all cylinders, working in the cognitive, creative, and emotional domains. When the pizza shop opened for business, developing the necessary language structures, with my help, happened naturally. Here's how the shop looked and sounded:

A waitress approaches the table and says, "Hello! Welcome to Delicious Pizza! How are you? What kind of pizza would you like today? You have a choice of three toppings: pepperoni, peppers, or mushrooms. Would you like a slice, or would you prefer to order a whole pizza?" (See Figure 5–14.) As customers respond, she records their request with checkmarks on a pizza ticket pulled from her apron. "Would you like a drink?" Again, she adds checkmarks to the ticket. (See Figure 5–15.)

Returning to the kitchen, the waitress gives the slip to the cashier, who adds up the items as the cook prepares the meal (see Figures 5–16 and 5–17). The kitchen bell rings, signaling that the order is ready for delivery. As the waitress serves the meal, she graciously leaves the check on a tip tray and says, "Thank you so much. When you're ready, please pay the cashier."

The cashier pushes beads across the abacus, adding up items, and enters the addition equation on the digital cash register, giving added numeration experience. "That will be six cents, please," says the cashier, who then collects the coins and puts them in the drawer. "Thank you. Please come again to Delicious Pizza! Have a nice day."

■ What We Can Learn

The dramatic play environment is a natural forum for integrating language and learning. By stopping to reflect on how to make play parallel the real world, a teacher opens opportunities for integration in writing, reading, math, language development, science, social studies, art, and music. As play becomes more purposeful, children deepen their understanding of the world and how it operates.

In creating stimulating play environments that simulate the real world, I aim to provide additional contexts for children to learn and explore. With the pizza shop, children understood why writing is important when they made signs, order tickets, and menus. (After the children designed and wrote the menu, I typed it, and they illustrated it.) They learned how addition and money function in everyday life when they operated as the cashier or the customer. They developed critical thinking and problem-solving skills when they figured out the restaurant's logistics or designed tables and chairs. Language structures particular to this setting expanded when students role-played a hostess, waiter, or waitress. Fine motor skills developed when they sewed pouches to hold money, and artistic expression was enhanced when they created delicious pizzas out of cardboard, paint, and tissue paper.

FIGURE 5–14 *Julia reads items from the menu to a customer.*

FIGURE 5–15 *Julia takes a pizza order.*

FIGURE 5–17 *Julia and Mona construct a homemade pizza to fill an order.*

FIGURE 5–16 *Mona totals pizza expenses on the cash register.*

Most of the aforementioned skills can also develop in many other dramatic play contexts, such as a veterinary clinic, grocery store, doughnut shop, beauty parlor, art gallery, or café. Encouraging the use of big blocks for creating a house, playground, or mall gives depth and breadth to the play environment. The same goes for combining play areas to make experiences more dynamic. For instance, after children create a grocery store, I might suggest building a playground or park out of big blocks. This addition becomes a post-shopping experience, fostering additional dynamic play.

Children respond to this kind of modeling and elicit others to work alongside their friends. As language structures become more complex to suit the situation, children gain confidence; actions become more decisive and focused. I'll hear the mommies sitting on a bench, rocking their babies, conversing with one another about the sale on bananas at the local store or what they plan to make for dinner.

By listening and observing, teachers have an opportunity to create new learning constructs for children within the creative domain. Tyrus' brainstorm that our pizza shop needed a play area led to so many more ideas. I could suggest designing an entire play section, housed in small blocks, for waiting customers. Math manipulatives, puzzles, books, or play dough might be added to this environment. Children could play in this area before or after their meal at Delicious Pizza!

Highly structured play like the pizza shop serves a different purpose from allowing children to freely build and play without prescribed goals. Children benefit from both. Explicit play instruction maximizes content integration, while experimenting and exploring without parameters fosters self-discovery. The pizza shop offered opportunities to integrate specific content as mentioned earlier, while the store (which I talk about in the following section) and Tyrus' play area exemplified natural synergy. In those examples of free play, I was not the director; the children led the way.

In our classroom, the workbench, water table, easel, art area, classroom animals, science table, and writing area provide additional learning opportunities for children—for example, building abstract sculptures (see Figure 5–18) or investigating volume and fluid dynamics. All help develop critical thinking, boost self-esteem, and ensure that children are learning in all three domains: cognitive, creative, and emotional.

■ Less Control, More Creativity

Creativity breeds creativity. Over years of teaching and observing choice time, I've come to appreciate how different groups of children, using the same materials, can create a myriad of unique artifacts limited only by their varied imaginations. The most exciting part is watching them build on one another's ideas. One child does something, and suddenly, focus shifts and enthusiasm builds; others embark on a

FIGURE 5–18 *Julia holds her completed workbench project.*

mission. Ideas start to piggyback on one another, and creations become more sophisticated.

One day, for example, Giovanni began experimenting with paper animal constructions. He made a menagerie of zoo animals by cutting, gluing, and stapling body parts together and adding marker details. With suggestions, he created jungle grass by cutting thin strips into lime green construction paper and curling the ends. We assembled these animals and taped the jungle scene to the wall above the listening center. Shannon and several others were inspired by Giovanni and added a spotted giraffe poking its head toward the sky, a tiger creeping through the grass, and an elephant trumpeting to the scene.

Around the same time, Abdili began constructing a series of functional paper masks by cutting holes for eyes, nose, and mouth and stapling a long rectangular strip of paper on the back as a strap. Once again, this spurred Tyrus and other children to join Abdili in his new exploration. Just observing his finesse with cutting paper and design was enough to draw anyone's attention. His classmates wanted to make a mask they could wear, too.

Creativity is not a one-way process; it's stunted when the teacher holds all the keys. Greater possibilities and opportunities for learning can surface only when teachers relinquish their focused instruction and allow free rein for more "messy" learning. Sometimes the mess is quite literal, as in the following story.

One day in the big-block area, children were constructing walls and a counter-top when suddenly a surge of energy took hold: Let's make a store! Within seconds, the builders had grabbed the cash register with its cache of coins from the math area and brought it and several tubs of math manipulatives over to the block area. No one asked for help, and before I knew it, *all* of the math manipulatives were lining the store shelves, ready for sale. Money was everywhere, and quickly the pattern blocks were mixed with the linking cubes, and little plastic animals were mixed in with colored math rods.

I smiled at the imagination even as I cringed at the chaos. The children's play was quite intentional. They were making a mess, but it was a mess with a purpose, which is why I stood back and let it go. I learn so much when I allow children's interests to take the lead. If I had intervened, I would have squashed the enthusiasm and momentum. Their idea was brilliant, and they were showing me what to do next. The children needed support to organize a system for running the store: how to carry sale items, where to put money, how to choose who would be the cashier, how to return purchases. So we talked at great length about the logistics and brain-stormed ways to help the store run smoothly.

Letting go of control can be a scary process for a teacher; you don't know what the children might do. Teachers need to repeatedly model and state expected behaviors until the room is running the way they desire. The store was a wonderful opportunity for me to support the children in executing their own ideas, rather than mine, more efficiently.

■ Outdoor Play: Get Your Wiggles Out

"Wee! Yeah!" Shouts and giggles erupt as the kids blast full speed toward the playground. "Mrs. Kempton, come see me do the ringers!" Charles shouts with great enthusiasm.

"Wow! You can get across all by yourself now, without any help?"

"Yeah!" He beams. I watch as Charles skillfully maneuvers one hand at a time, swinging his hips in perfect synchronicity.

Nearby, Tafaris is staring glumly as his friend accomplishes this pass. "Do you want a boost, sweetheart?" I ask. He reluctantly nods, and I hoist him up. A smile spreads across his face as he grabs the first bar. "Remember how Charles reached forward with each hand and swung his hips? That gave him power. It's all in the hips, honey!" With minimal support, Tafaris propels his body forward with gusto.

Whenever possible, barring rain or snow, we go outside to play. Fresh air, a shift in focus, running, skipping, climbing, jumping rope, laughing, and shouting without classroom restrictions all have an amazing effect on children. When given a physical outlet, children are better able to accommodate cognitive work. A gross motor break between writing and reading workshop provides a balanced day, helping children to remain content and focused during the quieter periods.

Physical activity is critical in strengthening a child's attitude and sharpening focus. The mind accommodates additional information better when it gets regular breaks for physical activity.

Both Charles and Tafaris showed a significant shift in attitude after they'd displayed their prowess on the ringers. Returning to the classroom with pride and confidence, they were refreshed, focused, and ready to learn.

■ Where to Start

- Observe what children do with play materials, and look for opportunities to build on their ideas.
- Continually peruse catalogs with an eye out for items that expand critical thinking and discovery or could enhance a play area (e.g., cash register, abacus, shopping carts, marble chutes).
- Order specific materials, or gather ones easily acquired, to enhance the children's play.
- Pool part of your classroom budget with a colleague's, and order expensive items that can then be rotated and shared.
- Try combining different environments, making play more dynamic and interactive.
- Think about how you could integrate more writing, reading, math, art, music, science, and language into play.

Write to Read

The fastest way to teach a child to read is to teach them to write.

—Mem Fox

F avi hunched over her daybook, crayons moving intently. From what I could see through her long, straight brown hair, she was drawing a small stick figure lying in the middle of an enormous bed. Using crayons in carefully selected colors, she sprinkled bright confetti all around her illustration. It was priceless!

Drawing is often the place where children's stories begin, and I was curious to know the story behind Favi's picture. I approached her side and knelt down. "So what are you writing about, sweetheart?"

"My bed," she responded shyly.

"What *about* your bed?"

In a tiny voice, still hiding behind her hair: "I got a bed."

"Is it new?" I asked.

She nodded slowly.

"You got a new bed? How exciting! Tell me about it, honey. What does it look like?"

Silent stare.

"What color is it?"

"White," she answered tentatively.

"Wow—so you got a new white bed! Tell me some more about it; tell me about the size . . ." I purposely let this trail off open-ended, not wanting to put words into her mouth.

Silence.

"Can you show me with your hands what it looks like?" Movement often helps get kindergartners talking.

Favi stretched her arms wide apart. A huge smile spread across her face as she said a single word: "*Big.*"

I carefully restated what we knew so far: "So you got a new big white bed, Favi! Let's write that down. Quick, get your pencil, sweetheart. What do you hear? *I . . .*" She carefully wrote an *I* on her paper and looked up at me for further support.

"Say *got* slowly. What sound do you hear at the beginning?" She formed a *G* on her paper. She put it too close to the letter *I*, but that didn't matter. Early in the school year I'm not concerned about spacing or even about all the sounds in a word; I want students to put their thoughts down on paper as quickly as possible and not get bogged down in mechanics.

"Do you hear something at the end of the word? Listen closely." I pronounced *got* again, putting exaggerated emphasis on the *t.*

Favi nodded and wrote a *T.* We continued methodically stretching out beginning and ending sounds together, always rereading the words on the paper before adding new ones. (See the section "Writing on the Message Board" later in this chapter for a further description of how to stretch out words with children.)

I asked Favi to share her story in the author's chair, a brightly colored hand-painted gift from one of my former kindergartners. The author's chair, at the front of our oval, is where all my budding writers share their precious stories. It is also the special place where I sit during group time. With gentle coaxing, she reluctantly agreed.

"Favi, was this your first bed?" I asked after she'd read her story to the group.

Her eyes twinkled as she gently smiled and nodded.

"Wow—what a big girl you are to have a bed all to yourself! How special!" Tenderly I continued the inquiry. "So where did you sleep before, sweetheart?"

"My grandma," she softly responded.

I smiled as tears filled my eyes. The image of Favi snuggled close to Grandma in bed over the years is still embedded in my mind, a tender reflection of love.

▨ Talking to Formulate What to Write, Writing to Preserve What We Say

Favi's story is a simple, precious example of why we write: to capture and remember experiences that matter. For children, the process starts with speaking: quality talk leads to rich written work. For the teacher, it begins with listening, paying careful attention to a child's thoughts so that you can gently elicit important details, restate ideas so they're not forgotten, provide words when necessary, and connect talk to paper, making the talk permanent.

The cognitive, creative, and emotional domains are the lenses through which I look and listen when conferring with a child. In Favi's conference, I was operating from the cognitive domain in asking for details about her bed: "Is it new? What does it look like? What color? Tell me about the size." We had recently launched into using mental images as a comprehension strategy, so Favi was beginning to understand how writers use rich language to pull readers into a story.

I added the emotional lens when I continued the inquiry: "Was this your first bed? Where did you sleep before?" Usually one or two of the domains take precedence during any given conference. For instance, in this case it was enough to encourage Favi to write the basic facts about her bed. Another conference focusing on the emotional domain might have yielded some writing about her grandmother.

First, however, Favi would have had to explore how she felt about the change in her sleeping arrangements. Like any of us, children can write only when they get in touch with what they think and feel. The process is endlessly circular: Thoughts and feelings inform writing and speaking, and writing and speaking bring forth new thoughts and feelings. As George Sheehan (n.d.) put it, "Until we say it or write it down, we are unaware of what is actually at the root of our lives."

So "Write it down; I love the way you said that!" becomes my mantra each year as I grow new writers in my classroom. Slowly, through writing, a child's expressed thoughts become visible and concrete. As children write, they build stronger connections to the language wheel. Most are already comfortable with the language wheel: "What we *think*, we can *say*." Next comes "What we *say*, we can *write*." And then "What we *write*, we can *read*."

Writing and reading go hand in hand, but for me, writing clearly comes before reading. Thirty-plus years of research show that immersing children in writing is the most developmentally appropriate first step toward the goal of reading. Almost all the beginning skills a child needs to master in reading can be developed through the writing process (Bissex 1980). My own experience backs up that research.

I teach reading through writing because writing teaches children so many reading skills:

- letters and sounds
- conventions of print: left-to-right progression (directionality), return sweep, voice-print match, punctuation, spacing
- significance of illustrations, role of detail and color
- importance of rereading

During the first half of the year, I emphasize skill instruction in writing workshop and leave reading workshop for children to practice those skills independently. The skills include sliding a finger from left to right under both known words (referred to as "familiar islands") and unknown words; identifying small sight words by landing on familiar islands; paying close attention to beginning and ending sounds; and noticing spacing and punctuation. I deliberately weight the balance heavily on the side of writing earlier in the year, then add more reading time as the year progresses, introducing advanced skills such as how to figure out an unknown word or read with fluency.

Here's a look at how I organize my teaching of writing: the various segments of the day, the roles that children and teacher play in the process, and how the three domains advance learning.

◼ Writing Workshop

Writing workshop has three vital components: a minilesson, guided independent practice (where children record their thoughts through pictures, letter strings, and words in journals or story folders), and an author's share. These three components directly relate to and support one another.

Minilessons: Modeled Writing

We begin the year by talking about authors and illustrators, who they are and where they get ideas for writing stories. Children easily understand this concept when explained: authors write what they know and care about. So I start the year modeling my knowledge and love of bunnies—how I've raised them since I was a little girl, what they eat, where they live, how they behave. My talk gives children repeated exposure to oral storytelling. Then I link oral language to the printed page, using pictures to compose a one-page story about Floppy, our classroom bunny.

The next day, I retell my story, adding details and color that I intentionally left out the first time. First I do this through drawing, for instance, by coloring the bunny on my paper gray and adding movement lines to show him jumping. Then I introduce how to tell a story through both pictures and words. After describing Floppy and his behavior, I share with them what I love most: "Floppy loves to run around and kick his legs in the air!" I write the words on the lines below my illustration.

The first time I model writing, I explain to the children that writing is hard work, so I'm going to do my very best job putting down the letters I hear. I'm clear with them that the way *they* write words will be different from the way adults spell. "You're just beginning to write, and your writing is not going to look like adult writing." I model stretching out words, omitting some, and representing most with just the beginning letter. *Floppy likes to run around and kick his legs in the air!* becomes "FLTRAKHLNR!" I reread my writing proudly, tracking letters from left to right, and introduce the function of the exclamation point.

These initial one-letter representations of words for story writing convey a clear message: you can do this, too. Soon I start talking about spacing as well. After the first month of school, when the children have some letters under their belts, correct spelling comes into play. If most children in your class arrive already knowing the letters and sounds, you can accelerate the process.

"All of you are authors and illustrators," the children hear constantly from me. I elicit verbal stories about what they know and care about (pets, family, favorite activities) and encourage them to write about these important people and experiences. Before heading to their seats to write, students first share their thoughts with a partner. When children are unable to generate an idea, I remind them of an experience they shared with me or the class. I continually plant these seeds, reinforcing the notion that we write what we know and care about.

In writing workshop at the beginning of the year, wordless books powerfully demonstrate how authors and illustrators tell stories through pictures. During the first month of school I read and reference this literature, emphasizing that beautifully detailed illustrations help readers experience the richness of a story. (See Chapter 8 for titles of wordless books.) Children's stories quickly progress from a single illustration to a picture with a string of random letters, numbers, or squiggles that aim to explain it. Anahi's sweet story about her dolly is an example of this emerging stage (see Figure 6–1).

As the year advances, modeled writing expands, matching the expectations for what children will achieve in skill and content. These skills are strategically incorporated at various points in the year during modeled writing exercises (see Table 6–1).

The introduction of writing skills follows no prescribed time line; it all depends on your students' abilities. To a child already reading fluently, for example, you might introduce most of the early skills in the first month of school. If you have a few children at this level, form a small group at the beginning of writing time for quick skill introduction. When children begin telling stories with detailed pictures and "words" (random letters), I introduce skills (stretching out sounds, leaving spaces) appropriate to their level. I reflect on what the top half of my class needs to guide my instructional timing. I teach to the highest end, elevating language and thinking while carefully scaffolding skills for my younger or less experienced writers.

Here's what I want my children to be able to do by the end of the year:

- comprehend the purpose and function of writing
- identify where stories come from
- generate stories through pictures and words
- stretch out thoughts independently (three or more sentences)
- understand the function and purpose of punctuation and use it in writing
- use spaces

FIGURE 6–1 *Anahi's story:* I was crying when my dolly broke.

- identify at least eighteen sight words
- incorporate known sight words in their writing
- experiment with rich language
- try different genres (letters, poetry, how-to, etc.)
- most of all, love writing!

I informally evaluate progress on a daily basis, carefully observing how children work independently, using the print that surrounds them (e.g., books, charts, signs, labels) for spelling and peers for support. Keeping your long-term goals for writing in mind helps you assess children's progress toward those goals from day to day.

Minilessons: Read-Alouds

Our writing minilesson often begins with a read-aloud. I choose the text based on one of the four comprehension strategies I focus on in kindergarten: activating schema, creating mental images, questioning, or inferring (Keene and Zimmermann 1997).

Skill	Beginning	Middle	End
TABLE 6–1 *Modeled Writing Skills*			
Drawing: the importance of color and detail	x	x	x
Rereading	x	x	x
How to read pictures in fiction and nonfiction—what it looks and sounds like	x		
Difference between letters and numbers (Letters are used to communicate words.)	x		
Matching text with illustration	x		
Stretching out sounds	x	x	x
Talking and thinking bubbles	x		
Beginning sounds of words	x		
Punctuation (purpose and function)	x	x	
Using *-ing*	x	x	
Cross-outs	x	x	
Arrows	x	x	
Beginning and ending sounds of words	x	x	
Beginning, middle, and ending sounds of words		x	x
Complete thoughts	x	x	x
Spacing between words		x	x
Incorporating known sight words (for more skilled writers)	x	x	x
Difference between a letter and a word	x	x	
Incorporating rich language		x	x
Expansion of thought (for more skilled writers)		x	x
Personal reflection (for more skilled writers)		x	x
Questioning (embedded questions)		x	x
Inference (showing versus telling) through pictures and words; making writing more interesting		x	x
Lengthening personal narratives to include beginning, middle, and end of stories		x	x
Poetry		x	x
Letters		x	x
Books (personal narratives, fictional, pattern, how-to)		x	x

Read-alouds strengthen listening comprehension, reveal readers' thinking processes, and model how to apply comprehension strategies in writing.

So, for instance, if my focus is activating schema (using background knowledge to deepen comprehension), I choose a book like *Bailey the Big Bully* (Boyd 1989) to read aloud. Before I read, I ask the children who bullies are and what they do. If this talk shows gaps in their schema, I add detail, building a solid foundation of background knowledge so that they'll be able to appreciate the value of this strategy when they hear the story.

My questions tap the cognitive domain, but of course the answers move into the emotional domain as children relate their experiences with bullies. "Hold onto those thoughts and feelings," I tell them. "You may want to write about them after the story." A few of the children act on this suggestion during writing workshop.

The next day, before rereading *Bailey the Big Bully*, I share with children a bullying experience I had when I was a little girl at summer camp. "I know how the children feel in this story when Bailey orders them around by telling them to give him their cookies, or to go get the ball when it flies over the fence, because I have been bullied. It's really terrifying! When I think about what I know and what it reminds me of, that helps me better understand the story." After the read-aloud, I connect strategies to written work by suggesting that the children think about a time when someone was being mean to them or ordered them around.

I retell my experience the following day and model writing, recording the summer camp story with both pictures and words. The children once again experience the reciprocity of language:

What we *think* we can *say*.
What we *say* we can *write*.
What we *write* we can *read*.

(Linking comprehension strategies to written work is further discussed in Chapter 7.)

Minilessons take many forms. Ideas come from careful listening, observing children's writing, and identifying needs. For example, when I conferred with Isabella, she had already written "I SBLE," meaning *I saw a bully*. "What a great start you have!" I told her. "Let's reread this." As we read, Isabella noticed that she'd actually written *I saw bully*; she'd left out the article *a*. "Remember we talked about how writers use arrows to stick in a word they missed?" I asked. "I think you might need one here." She nodded in agreement, traced over the faint arrow I'd drawn on her paper, and inserted the *A*.

"So what happened when you saw the bully?"

"She said, 'Give me your cookies!'" Isabella quietly replied. I helped her with the spacing and with stretching out the sounds of the words to write her story. "Let's

FIGURE 6–2 *Isabella's bully story:* I saw a bully. She said, "Give me your cookies!" "I'm going to eat my own cookies!"

reread, sweetheart. You saw a bully who wanted your cookies. And what did *you* say?"

"I'm going to eat my own cookies!" Isabella responded defiantly as she started adding the response to her story.

"Why don't you put one of those . . ."

Before I completed my thought, she interjected, "A talking bubble!" and drew a big oval from the open mouth of each girl in her illustration. I left her to independently include the dialogue between herself and the bully (see Figure 6–2).

When a child innocently omits a pertinent word from a text, that's the perfect time to teach the importance of arrows and how they function. Often this new learning is presented at the end of writing workshop during the author's share because a child has just experimented with arrows and wants to share this great discovery right away. Author's share can involve a child either reinforcing a skill I've demonstrated to the class or introducing a new concept. When Isabella shared in the author's chair, her friends learned not just about the purposes of arrows, spaces, and talking bubbles but also about extending an experience and making personal connections to a text.

Sometimes I choose a child's writing to launch our writing workshop. If, for example, we're working on spacing and several children are doing it well, but we haven't had time for all of them to share, I have them present their work the following morning in a minilesson. Often I stop a workshop midstream to exhibit a child's writing, demonstrating a skill I want everyone to be reminded of (adding color and detail, using rich words, etc.).

"Would all of you look up here? Notice the great detail and color Gina used in her illustration. I feel like I'm right there in her mouth. I can feel her tooth wiggling just through her illustration. . . . Do you also notice how big her face is? It's just like Ted Rand drew in *Salt Hands*; remember the close-up illustration of the deer with the little girl? He purposely drew the deer large to make us feel like we were right there! Guys, remember the importance of adding color and detail. Slow down with your drawings, and think like a reader. Remember how great illustrations make you feel more part of a story." (See Figure 6–3.)

Another short interruption: "Look at all the great writing Julia did on her own. Think about telling your story through pictures and words today, just like Julia did. Try picking up your pencil and stretching out sounds on your own. I know it's scary, but I want you to try it anyway. If you get stuck, remember to ask the friends at your table for help if I'm not there. You can just say, 'Tyrus, do you know what letter makes a *guh* sound?' or 'I forgot how to make an *m*.' If someone asks you for help, show them how to form the letter in the air or with your finger on the table. Remember not to write it in their daybook for them; good teachers always *show*."

Guided Independent Practice

Classroom daybooks (journals) are set in a tub at child height near our writing tables, for easy access at all times of the day. Daybooks are twenty or so sheets of paper with a construction paper cover, stapled together on the left side. Each page has an empty space at the top for illustrations and black lines at the bottom for writing. These sheets are premade with black marker and duplicated. As the year progresses, additional lines allow for more writing and individualizing.

Before writing workshop, I spread the children's daybooks out at assigned tables

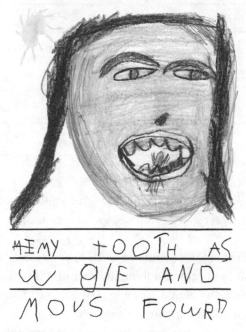

AAVO
AND BAK!

MEMY tOOTH AS
w giE AND
MOVS FOWRD

FIGURE 6–3 *Gina's piece:* My tooth is wiggly and moves forward and back!

so that everyone will have immediate access after the minilesson. I assign children to tables based on strengths, weaknesses, and behavior. Having a predictable set of friends and procedures fosters efficiency, independence, and risk taking. Once the children have gotten comfortable with the arrangements, I change the seating plan during the year, making the dynamics richer.

Sound cards in the center of each table serve as references to help children quickly locate which letter is associated with a sound. The City Sounds cards (Lusche 2003) associate a picture, sound, and movement with each letter, giving children multiple ways to remember (other visual, auditory, and kinesthetic letter-sound systems can be equally effective). I introduce the sounds and movements in the first few weeks of school; each sound card has a short rhyme for the letter as well. I teach the sounds out of sequence, focusing on easily distinguishable phonemes like *r*, *s*, and *d*. So, for instance, *r* is the angry dog sound. Children get on all fours and mimic the sound of a feisty dog: *Rrrr! S* is the hissing tire sound. Children form their hands in a circle like a tire while slowly compressing their fingers together and making the sound of air escaping: *Ssss!*

Also on each table, children find a community basket of crayons and large-diameter pencils. The pencils have no erasers. When young children are beginning to write, it's important that they focus on putting their thoughts on paper as quickly as

TABLE 6–2 *Word Card*			
I can it the at	a on in like he	to and my you dog	go is look up see
am	we	me	this

possibly without worrying about mistakes. I model for children how to simply draw a line through any unwanted writing and continue with the thought. This not only communicates, "Let's not worry about mistakes," but emphasizes the importance of saving one's thinking.

After several months of writing workshop, I put laminated cards in pencil cans on the writing table for those children who are beginning to identify words. The cards list the words tested on the DRA 2 (Developmental Reading Assessment) Task 9 assessment (Beaver 2005), as well as four additional words. (See Table 6–2.)

When a child can identify a sight word on their list, I punch a hole beside that word on the card. Children are responsible for spelling words correctly in their writing once they recognize them, so the cards serve as a good quick reference (see Figure 6–4).

I use the word cards as a teaching tool. For example, as Mireya and I reread the writing in her daybook, I say, "Mireya, see the word we just stretched out together, *a-n-d*? It says *and*. That's a word you know how to write, and very soon you're going to be reading it! Look, sweetheart." I point to the *and* on her word card. "This says *and*, *a-n-d*. . . . Tell me when you think you know that word."

I don't punch a hole next to a word on the card until the child informs me that she can identify it. First I quickly remove the card from sight and ask the student to spell the word; if she can, I punch the card. Then I help her practice identifying the word. After punching *and* on Mireya's card, I said, "Mireya, during reading time today, let's read *The Seed Song* together. It has lots of *and*s in it; let's see if we can find them."

Soft instrumental music plays in the background while the children write and my paraprofessional and I confer with them. This background music helps focus the children and keep them calm and centered. "If we can't hear the beautiful music, then it's too loud and you need to lower your voices," I tell them.

I encourage children to experiment with the focus of the minilesson in their writing, but I don't expect every child to be ready to apply every skill, even with guided support. For example, a child who can identify only a few letters isn't ready to work

FIGURE 6–4 *Conferring with Ragat during writing workshop*

on transferring sight words into his writing, and a child just beginning to stretch out words isn't ready to focus on expanding a thought. It's important to look at each child individually. Should one child focus more on detail because his illustrations are difficult to decipher? Does another need to slow down and start thinking about adding spaces? Is this child ready to start taking risks with stretching out sounds? Could that one start expanding her writing by adding a reflection or question?

SMALL-GROUP SUPPORT

Roughly half my students enter school with little experience in letters, sounds, or numeral identification. As school proceeds, it quickly becomes apparent who will need more instruction and guidance. The majority of the children acquire the sounds of the alphabet within the first month of school and can identify 90 percent of the letters, both upper- and lowercase, by midyear or sooner. Incorporating movement substantially increases the kids' new learning and retention.

Still, within the first two months of school, I usually notice five or six children who need daily support in writing. Instead of spreading them among the other children, I have found it's a more efficient use of time and energy to group them. As I confer with the majority of the class during writing workshop, my paraprofessional, under my supervision, supports this small group of our youngest, most inexperienced learners at a separate table. If I had no paraprofessional, I would train a parent to support this group.

Grouping children who need more direct support decreases the student-to-teacher ratio and allows more individualized instruction to the writers who need it most. Meanwhile, I support the majority of the class, stimulating and nudging my mature thinkers and learners. The small group is in no way separate or alienated from

FIGURE 6–5 *My paraprofessional and I confer with students during writing workshop.*

the rest of the children; all of our writing tables are only an arm's length apart. My paraprofessional sits at the small-group table while I confer among the remaining four tables. (See Figure 6–5.)

At the beginning of the year, I model behavioral aspects of small-group writing for my paraprofessional. Since Ms. Lisa, another paraprofessional who took over for Ms. Natalie, is with me for half the day, I communicate with her before school and throughout the morning, directing her in specific instructional objectives for the children. We take a few minutes during lunch to assess the results from the small-group interaction while setting a direction for the next day. If we don't have time to review the morning, a quick summation after writing time (as children are transitioning to the author's chair) is usually enough.

Both Ms. Lisa and I introduce skills to groups in ways that draw all children into active participation. So as she supports Tafaris in stretching out the word *went*, she asks him, "What letter makes the *wuh* sound?" No response. "Guys, can you help Tafaris find the letter that makes this sound?" She models and prompts the children to reenact the movement of a sponge sliding back and forth across a window (window washing) with her as she reinforces the sound and names the letter ("*Wuh, wuh, w.*"). The children enthusiastically point to the picture and letter on their sound cards. This group interaction is empowering for the children who already know the skill and reinforcing for ones who need more repetition.

Working with a paraprofessional requires close communication. I am clear with her about my expectations, wanting her to closely examine the language I use with children at every possible moment. When introducing a new strategy or personal intervention, such as how to use your words, I stop my instruction and ask my paraprofessional to join us to watch and listen. This may happen during a modeled writing exercise, in the middle of our writing workshop, or during shared reading with a big book.

The closeness of our writing tables aids communication. "Uvaldo, you wrote a great story today!" the paraprofessional says to a member of her small group. "I can't believe the awesome job you did with your illustration, and how you stretched out all those words. Mrs. Kempton, Uvaldo knows how to spell the word *and*!" Comments like these let me know how a child is doing and give me a chance to acknowledge that child, perhaps by choosing him to share in the author's chair.

When a new child enters the class after the school year has started, I assess her and, if needed, place her in my paraprofessional's group. She gives direct support until the child acquires skills and independence. If a child is lacking letter identification and sounds, she pulls this child aside first thing in the morning and works with him briefly on sounds and movements associated with letters, taken from the letter-sound system found in *No More Letter of the Week* (Lusche 2003). Having a common system of sounds and movements associated with letters is important for late arrivals, providing them a support tool during writing. For example, the sound card for the letter *h* shows an out-of-breath runner crossing the finish line, panting with a *huh* sound. A child from another school probably wouldn't understand this reference because she wouldn't know the sound associated with the picture.

Children move in and out of the small group depending on their needs. Sometimes after a few weeks of direct support in stretching out sounds, for example, they are ready to join the rest of the class, reflecting a new independence.

FOLLOW-UP MINILESSONS

This list shows the areas in which students often need additional support after the whole group is introduced to skills during a minilesson. My paraprofessional reinforces the skills in follow-up lessons with the small group (see Table 6–3).

Author's Share: Learning from Others

Our writing time ends with two children sharing their written work in the author's chair while the rest of the class listens intently. Modeling how to listen as a respectful audience starts in the first month of school, during community share time on the oval, and continues throughout the year. Author's share represents a slight shift in

TABLE 6–3 *Follow-Up Minilessons*

Skills/Minilessons	Beginning	Middle	End
Emphasize telling stories through pictures with color and detail	x	x	x
Support children in drawing; demonstrate how to draw a person, a tree, or a house with basic shapes	x		
Model for children how to articulate thoughts in complete sentences that make sense	x	x	x
Encourage children to stretch out sounds in a series of words and record their thinking as a complete thought	x	x	x
Reinforce the names and sounds associated with letters	x	x	x
Draw letters in the air or on the table with a finger, reinforcing proper formation; if necessary, get behind a child and gently hold her hand as she forms letters	x	x	
Assess and support children to create attainable goals; make unknown information explicit to children (e.g., a letter name or word they can't identify)	x	x	x
Encourage letter formation and penmanship on dry-erase boards (occasionally)		x	x
Support children with spacing; scaffold this process by encouraging them to use their two fingers or draw light lines defining where words should be written; prior to drawing these lines, rehearse orally how many words need to be written		x	x
Increase writing expectation by extending a thought		x	x
Model for children how to use resources around them (e.g., books, labels, signs) to find words they need to spell, always linking print they are reading to writing		x	x
Encourage children to use lowercase letters in their writing		x	x

the context of community because rather than sitting around the oval, the children sit inside it, facing the author. The setup works because they're engaging more with one child than with one another.

The author sitting in the hand-painted chair begins by freely describing an experience he's written about. I hold his daybook so others can easily view his writing. First I ask him to tell his story through his illustration (this requires continual modeling), providing the class with a chance to develop language, read pictures, and emphasize the importance of color and detail. Next we move everyone's attention

FIGURE 6–6 *Ragat shares his work in the author's chair.*

from the picture to the writing. The author rereads his piece, tracking words (frequently with my support), and then I read it as well. Echoing a child's language lets the others hear his thinking clearly and gives the author an opportunity to hear his own voice (see Figure 6–6).

Most of the time, I choose the authors specifically to reinforce the focus of the minilesson. But sometimes the author's chair is occupied by a child in need of recognition, or someone who has made a sudden leap in writing development, or a child who has experimented with a new skill unrelated to the minilesson (punctuation, use of an arrow to insert a new word, etc.). Take advantage of these precious learning moments in lieu of an agenda.

Whenever possible, I parallel a child's work with a published writer. For example, Noehlie (*NO-el-ee*) had written, "Me ANd iSABellA ARe PAliNG tARBAl, Waking the BAl! the Bal is seWiNG A RAND AND A RAND AND RAND the Pol!" (*Me and Isabella are playing tetherball, whacking the ball! The ball is swinging around and around and around the pole!*). After she shared her story, I ended the author's share with "Noehlie, I love how you described you and Isabella playing tetherball. You didn't just say you were hitting the ball, but you said . . ."

Noehlie finished this thought: "*Whacking* the ball!"

the Bal IS SeWing
A RAND AND A RAND
AND RAND the Pol!

Me AND ISABClla
ARe PAIING tARBAl,
WaKiAg the Bal!

FIGURE 6–7 *Noehlie's tetherball story*

"And, you didn't just say, 'The ball is swinging,' but you said, 'It is . . .'"

"Swinging *around, and around, and around* the pole."

"Wow, we could see that ball flying and wrapping itself around the pole. Noehlie, you repeated your words three times and added movement lines just like A. Birnbaum in *Green Eyes*, when he described Green Eyes racing around the tree. You made us feel like were right there in your story." (See Figure 6–7.)

Providing children with opportunities to articulate their thinking honors their voices and strengthens the reciprocity between oral and written communication. In addition, the author's share lets children model literacy as teachers while it empowers them as learners.

▇ Additional Opportunities to Model Writing

Writing on the Message Board

In the morning, after we've all read the date on the dry-erase board, I ask everyone, "So what should we write about today?" This writing period is part of our morning oval ritual, where I write text we all compose from the morning's talk. As the year progresses and children build listening stamina, I involve them in the writing process through interactive writing, "an instructional context in which a teacher shares a pen—literally and figuratively—with a group of children as they collaboratively compose and construct a written message" (McCarrier, Pinnell, and Fountas 2000, 4). I keep this interaction brief so I don't lose anyone's interest.

Sometimes I use this group-written text to teach specific content and vocabulary. An example of building schema and expanding vocabulary was when we collectively wrote, "Elephants use their trunks to reach for leaves!" I illustrated two meanings for the word *trunk*, reinforcing the use of the word in context. Other times, I leave the writing open-ended and pursue the interests of the children, such as when Shannon lost her tooth and found two dollars from the tooth fairy in her backpack.

Recently when we launched into questioning as a comprehension strategy, the children were beginning to wonder about everything they encountered. Halvin was intrigued with a white owl he'd observed on a class field trip to the Denver Zoo. During writing workshop he recorded in his daybook, "WI DO OWLS STA AWAK DRING THE DA?" He was curious about this because we had had numerous discussions, and read several books, about nocturnal animals. Halvin knew owls were a member of this group, which should have meant they were more active at night.

I sent him to the library to carry out research with our media specialist. With her support, Halvin discovered that snow owls are in fact diurnal; they're more active during the day than at night. The children and I were finishing our share on the oval as he returned from the library. "So what did you discover, Halvin?"

"Diurnal!" he blurted out.

"What did you say?"

"Diurnal!"

"Wow, what a rich word! What does that mean?"

He responded, "Awake at daytime . . ."

"And what else, Halvin?" I asked.

"Owl sleeps at night." I had him state this new learning in a complete sentence, reinforcing proper language construction.

The children orally crafted our shared writing message, deciding it would state, "Halvin discovered the snow owl at the zoo is diurnal!" In order to start writing this on the board, I prompted everyone, "So what do you hear at the beginning of the sentence?"

"Huh . . . Halvin," the kids shouted out. "*H!*" I quickly put down an *H* and continued stretching out the sounds in his name.

"Ahh," the children chimed in. "*A.*"

"What else do you hear?"

"Ell. *L.*" As I stretched out sounds, the children quickly identified the letter associated with the phoneme and collectively responded.

"What do you hear at the end of Halvin's name?"

"*In!*" they exclaimed.

"How do you spell *in*?"

"*I-n!*"

"Wow, great job, guys!"

We continued this process with the rest of the sentence, skipping over difficult *r*-controlled vowels (like the *e* in *discover*); I simply inserted those quickly and moved on to the next clearly defined letter and sound. I make a point of introducing short vowels later, when the children become skilled in differentiating complicated phonemes. "Let's reread: 'Halvin discovered' . . . how do you spell *the*?"

"*T-h-e!*" the children exclaimed. Quickly I recorded *the*, reread it with the class, and continued stretching out our thought. Whenever sight words like *the* and *in* are incorporated in my modeled writing, I make a point of showing the children where to find these words on their sight-word cards.

As we assembled our sentence, I continually modeled rereading text each time a new word was added, using voice-print match while lengthening the written communication. This is the identical process children engage in when effectively writing. Young writers tend to lose track of where they left off, and when they do, they ramble on, omitting words and getting lost in their writing. Rereading is an effective strategy for finding a launching point for further writing, and thus it's a skill I continually reinforce throughout the year.

"So, what mark should we put at the end of this writing?" I asked.

"An exclamation point!" they shouted.

"Why do we want to put that mark instead of a period?"

"Because we're excited!"

"Yes, we are. This is a great discovery for Halvin. We need to put an exclamation point to show how important it is and how excited we are!" After we'd finished recording our sentence on the dry-erase board, I encouraged everyone to reread the entire message as my finger tracked the words. "Great job, guys!" Halvin later recorded this information in his daybook after completing the research.

The fact that snow owls are diurnal was new information for me as well. I love learning alongside children, and I let them know this. "Halvin, this is great; I'm so glad you did this research. I learned something new today, honey! I love that new word *diurnal*. Can you guys say that, diurnal?" The children repeated the word. "Wow!" I exclaimed. Halvin beamed.

Depending on the time of year and the attention span of the group, I teach different skills through the writing we carry out on the message board. In the previous example, my focus was to acknowledge Halvin's reflective process (cognitive domain) and the proud discovery he made. Building new schema, feeling proud, and develop-

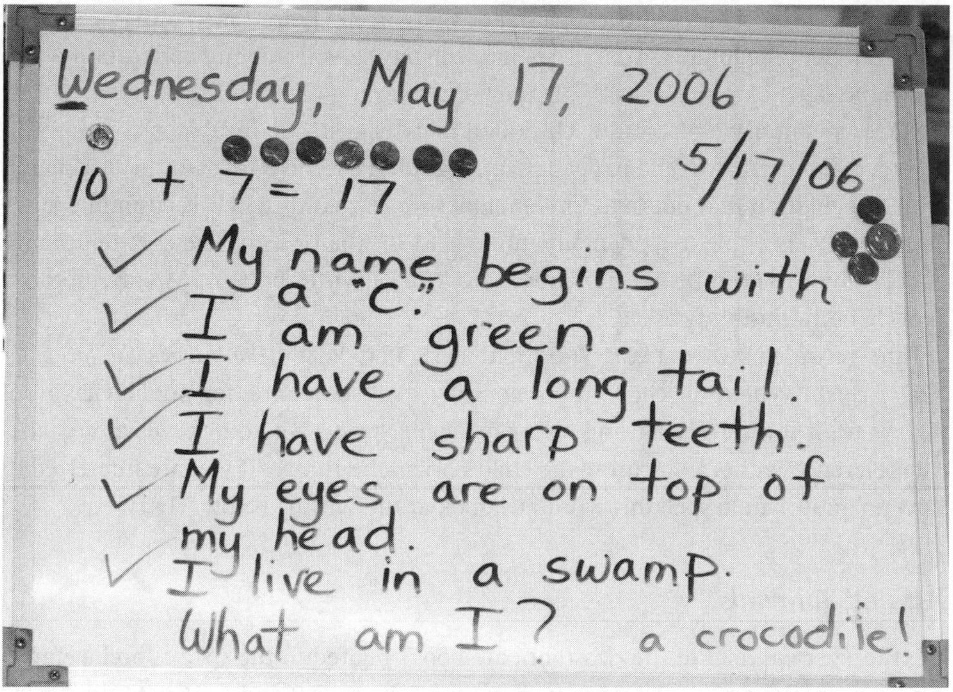

FIGURE 6–8 *Message board showing coin integration with date and riddle writing*

ing vocabulary for the class (creative and emotional domains) and reinforcing the process of writing were natural outcomes of the activity.

On another day, my intention might be to strengthen sight vocabulary, such as *the*, *at*, *me*, and *is*, by having children locate words on the board and circle them with a contrasting marker. Or my objective might be to make an announcement of something like an upcoming field trip, share something I've discovered, honor a child's birthday, or teach spelling patterns. Toward the end of the year, when I introduce riddles, children read the writing and infer the answer, and then we affirm each attribute with a checkmark to validate their thinking. (See Figure 6–8.)

Functional Writing

All writing has a purpose. Functional writing is writing with a *public* purpose, writing designed to communicate something specific to an audience. Signs, phone messages, and grocery lists are functional writing; they serve a much different purpose than does personal narrative or poetry. When introducing functional writing, I explain to the children the reason for making a sign for blocks like "Don't touch!" As the year progresses and small-block building becomes more sophisticated, I encourage children to keep their constructions out at the end of choice time so they can continue building the following day. They immediately see meaningful application when they tape signs onto their block constructions, warning others to stay away.

One day after we placed our chick and duck eggs in the incubator, a discussion emerged about what would happen if the eggs didn't receive constant heat. I shared with the children that our janitors sometimes unplug cords when vacuuming, and I wondered if they might accidentally unplug our incubator cord. The children immediately saw the need for functional writing. "Can I write the sign, Mrs. Kempton?" Jenecia enthusiastically asked.

She recorded, "DOT TACH The iNKUOATR PLG Pez!" (*Don't touch the incubator plug, please!*). Whenever children phonetically spell something for public viewing, I always print the correct spelling below in smaller print, where it serves as an accurate reference without obscuring the child's original writing. "If you are interested in how an adult would spell this word, just look at the writing below," I say.

Animal Journals

Next to every animal in the classroom are books related to the species and a simple bound journal for recording observations (see Figures 6–9 and 6–10). At the beginning of the year, when introducing the classroom, I discuss the function of these journals and model unique observations I have made. As part of a shared writing experience, I elicit the children's help in composing and recording what I've noticed, talk about the importance of dating an observation, and then choose a child to illustrate it.

After supporting children through the writing process, I encourage them to enter their own observations when they arise (see Figure 6–11). Students can write journals entries during writing workshop, choice time, or share time. I always make a point to share these anecdotal notes with the entire class, to promote more purposeful writing, emphasize the power in observation, and model thoughtful inquiry.

▧ What We Can Learn

It's important for children to understand the purpose of written communication and repeatedly hear the message "We write for a reason." Helping students understand *why* we write belongs at the forefront of our instruction. When we record questions about the world, we learn to pay close attention to life. Halvin's innate curiosity (cognitive domain) about the snow owl was the primary motivator for conducting his research. Then, taking charge of his learning through research, Halvin furthered his quest for understanding (cognitive domain). By recording his new learning that

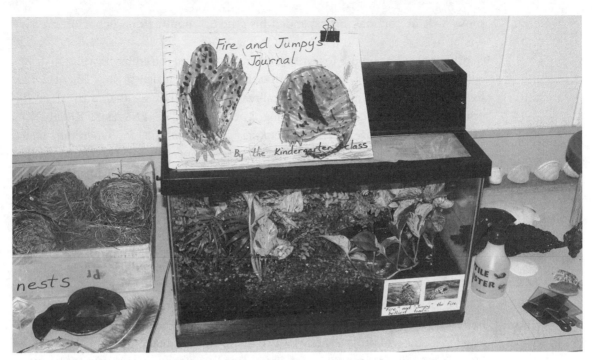

FIGURE 6–9 *Fire-bellied toads' aquarium and journal*

FIGURE 6–10 *Cajita's box and journal*

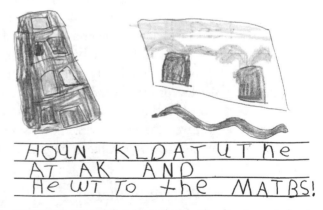

FIGURE 6–11 *Isabella's journal entry:* Houdinni crawled out of the tank and he went to the math tubs!

snow owls are diurnal, he expanded his schema about animal behavior (creative domain).

Children see a purpose for writing when they realize the embryos will stop developing if someone removes the plug and thus construct a sign saying, *Don't touch the incubator plug, please!* They write for real reasons when they see their artwork on the ground and post a sign nearby saying, "DONT TAK THE PNS PleS! KNDRGRDN ROOM 110" (*Don't take the pins, please! Kindergarten room 110*), and when they tape a sign to a block building stating, "DOT TCH!" (*Don't touch!*). Functional writing empowers children, capitalizing on the emotional domain. They learn that writing can have a direct effect on others; it causes change.

As they take on these projects, children learn about letters, sounds, and functions of print in contextually meaningful ways. All the writing examples in this chapter strengthen the relationships among the three domains within the contexts of writing and reading; they help with articulation of thoughts. Weaving the three domains together makes communication richer and more lasting.

In choosing what we'll write together on the dry-erase board, I reflect on the cognitive, creative, and emotional state of the class to determine the most significant activity in the moment. Shannon discovering how to make a giraffe by carefully observing Abdili's process; Fidencio discovering that elephants can swim under water with their trunks extended above the surface; and Lorraine missing her mom and dad, and feeling sad and lonely, became material for our interactive writing.

Focused writing activities, like the animal journals, take on different forms. If you're studying the metamorphosis of a caterpillar, you can keep a journal alongside the jar, promoting careful observation and recording of data. This idea can be expanded to the numerous insects children capture while out on the playground, or you might decide to record the most memorable events in the class over the course of the year, informally or more elaborately, in a hardbound notebook with plastic sleeves for writing and photographs. Notebooks such as these can become ongoing records of the work accomplished at the workbench or art area. Looking back on the year, reading our entries, the kids and I feel proud of all the work we've accomplished, particularly the growth in *writing*.

▤ Where to Start

- Evaluate general trends in assessment data within your classroom (e.g., identifying capital and lowercase letters, identifying beginning sounds in words, producing rhyming words, etc.). Which skills do most children have, and which do many lack?

- Focus subsequent instruction in the areas of need:

- Introduce a system of letter-sound recognition the first month of school.

- If most children can identify all letters and sounds, focus on supporting writing, stretching out sounds, and identifying simple sight words to incorporate in writing.

- Implement a writing workshop:

  - Emphasize telling personal experiences through pictures and words.

  - Have children record stories through pictures and random letter strings and, with modeling and support, put down letters associated with sounds.

- Model specific writing skills you want children to attain.

- Reflect on children's engagement during writing workshop, and focus instruction on the purpose of writing.

- Provide needed structure for struggling writers (e.g., small-group support, one-on-one instruction, scaffolds for skills such as how to draw, stretch out sounds, and leave spaces).

- Continually encourage and acknowledge children in front of others as they gain independence in writing. (Remember these are approximations and not perfect writing samples.)

- Provide support and model the next steps in writing to your advancing students.

- Reflect on where you could incorporate a shared writing experience during the day.

- Encourage functional writing, particularly during choice time (signs, notes, grocery lists, phone messages, etc.).

- Reflect on how to incorporate journals (e.g., animal, insect, classroom experiences) into your classroom.

7 | Thinking Strategies

To understand is to manipulate our own thinking.
—Ellin Keene

Teaching children to think. That, in essence, is our most important job—and what could be more exciting or more challenging? But *how* do you teach children to think? And, deeper still, how do you teach kids to think *about* their thinking?

To avoid feeling overwhelmed by the massiveness of this mission, I've learned to divide it into bite-size chunks. Over the years I've defined, labeled, and ordered the various thinking strategies most useful for kindergartners to learn. I've tackled this task diligently, as if strategies were as real and touchable as books to be alphabetized on a shelf. Because I view reading comprehension strategies as a subset of thinking strategies, I arrange the essential thinking strategies in specific ways designed both to enhance listening comprehension and to apply to writing.

We start with listening, for one simple reason: Kindergartners, especially early in the year, can understand much more complex texts than they can read. The books that my students can decode on their own—songbooks, pattern books, rhymes, leveled texts—are wonderful for their purpose, but they don't lend themselves well to talking about larger comprehension issues. So I read my class quality fiction and nonfiction that I've chosen to illustrate the particular strategy we're focusing on. Then I encourage the children to apply the strategy—both to their own writing and to their independent "rereading" (through pictures) of books they have chosen and ones I've read aloud.

I explicitly teach four thinking strategies defined by Keene and Zimmermann in *Mosaic of Thought* (1997)—*activating schema, creating mental images, questioning,* and *inferring*—and address the others (synthesizing, determining importance, monitoring for meaning) in context as they arise. To return to the image of the lenses, it's as if I'm flipping down a different lens for myself and the children in each six- or eight-week block devoted to a particular comprehension strategy. This month we look through the lens of activating schema, next month through the lens of questioning, and so on. Once I introduce a strategy, we do not set it aside and forget it. Rather, as each new strategy moves to the foreground, the others remain active in the background; we refer to them frequently. My careful ordering of these strategies, and selection of quality texts to illuminate each one, is something that other teachers can easily understand and implement or adapt for their own purposes.

The exciting part, however, is not the structure but the freedom. While in theory the strategies may seem as self-contained as books on a shelf, in practice teachers never address just one strategy in isolation from the others. Like many aspects of working with kindergartners, teaching thinking strategies illustrates a contradiction: structure, which sounds confining, actually winds up increasing flexibility—but only if you develop the confidence to follow where your students lead. By patiently flipping down the comprehension lenses one at a time, I help students gradually progress to a place where they can, quite suddenly and on their own, flip down several lenses at once, applying multiple strategies to think their way to new discoveries. That's the process of comprehension made visible.

To see what I mean, follow me through the story of Marty and his grandfather—but backward. We'll start with the amazing thinking and drawing that Marty did, then end with the lessons on thinking strategies that laid the foundation for his realizations. Before the day in question, I had worked with this group of kindergartners on two thinking strategies: *activating schema* and *creating mental images*. On the day that Marty drew his picture, we were in the midst of examining the strategy of questioning. But sticking with the lesson plan doesn't matter when a child is having a profound experience.

◼ Love from Above

The vehicle Marty was drawing—big door in back, red light on the roof—was clearly an ambulance. Just as clearly, the person lying on a stretcher being loaded inside, with a straight-line grimace on his face, was very hurt or very sick (see Figure 7–1). As we'd settled in that morning, Marty had been rereading *Nana Upstairs and Nana Downstairs* (1973), the classic Tomie dePaola book in which a child learns about death. We'd read the book as a class a few months before, and on this day I noticed Marty fondly flipping through the pages and staring at the illustrations.

Between what I knew of the book and what I could see in Marty's daybook illus-

FIGURE 7–1 *Marty's writing about his grandpa:* I will always be with you. I wonder if you can hear and see me?

tration, I approached him during writing workshop expecting to hear a sad connection to the story. I knew he had gained *some* insight, some new learning, just by observing his eyes and facial expression as he held the book. That day, at that moment, this book was *his*!

The class had been working for several weeks on questioning as a thinking strategy. But because his drawing showed that Marty had made some kind of deep personal connection with the book, activating schema was the lens I looked through as I bent to talk with him. "What are you writing about, sweetheart?" was all I needed to ask.

"My grandpa," Marty responded.

"Tell me about your picture," I said softly.

Using just a few words—"Last time, Grandpa . . ."—and pointing to the man on the stretcher, Marty filled in the most important blank.

"When you were reading *Nana Upstairs and Nana Downstairs*, were you reminded of Grandpa being taken away in the ambulance?" I asked gently.

Marty nodded silently.

Capturing that moment in language was foremost in my mind as I asked, "What do you remember about Grandpa? Did he say anything to you?"

Without hesitation, Marty responded, "I will always be with you." Grandpa had looked into his eyes and said those words as he was put into the ambulance.

"Wow," I said softly. "Marty, you've got to write that down."

Marty had been smiling as he'd shared this memory, so I knew he'd be OK with me continuing the inquiry. "What are you wondering about Grandpa?" I asked.

He was quiet for a few seconds. Then, at my suggestion, he brought *Nana Upstairs and Nana Downstairs* over to his writing table and flipped to the last illustration in the book, which shows Tommy grown up and a shooting star zooming across the sky. Marty's eyes lit up as a soft smile spread across his face. He thought of his grandpa, and he asked: "I wonder if you can hear and see me?"

"What would that look like, sweetheart? How could you show in your picture where Grandpa would be, if he could see and hear you?"

Without hesitating, Marty picked up his pencil and drew a figure at the top of the page, smiling and waving down. This was Grandpa, up in heaven.

Sometimes children can quite literally take your breath away. How much poorer would we all have been if, rather than following Marty's lead, I'd tried to direct his thinking to suit my plan for the day? I'd have risked letting him lose touch with his feelings about someone he loved. Later, in reflecting on this interaction, I understood that Marty had had this insight partly because I was there to support him, and partly because the work the class had been doing for weeks on questioning had primed his brain to think this way. As such, the moment represented a perfect microcosm of teaching: you painstakingly lay the foundation, then seize opportunities as they arise.

Watching Marty gaze intently at the pictures in *Nana Upstairs and Nana Downstairs* that morning touched me deeply because I could tell that something had touched him. I wondered what he saw in the illustrations, what they reminded him of. Wondering and feeling was the lens from which I listened and spoke with Marty. His pencil drawing quickly deepened my perspective and caused additional lenses to click into place. I could tell that he *had* made a deep connection, which stirred my passion to find out what that was. I began using questioning as a tool to draw out his background knowledge and get him to express new learning.

If I had not been there to ask, "What are you wondering about Grandpa?" Marty might not have continued thinking beyond the moment when Grandpa was taken away. If he hadn't asked his question about whether Grandpa could hear and see him, neither Marty nor I might ever have realized the depth of his reflections on death. And without Marty's question, I would not have been able to ask the next question, the one that allowed him to *show* his ideas on paper. Helping Marty capture his grandpa's last words, and his own big question, was empowering work that made his experience permanent.

Marty's pencil drawing of Grandpa smiling and waving down from heaven says it all. It still gives me goose bumps whenever I look at it. Marty was at peace because he knew his grandpa would always be with him and he would always be with his grandpa. This was a synthesis for Marty, new learning about relationships and loss.

■ Strategies: A Foundation of Four

For many children, kindergarten is their first experience with writing. Not only are they grappling with the logistics of paper, pencils, and crayons, but they're just beginning to understand the *purpose* for using these tools. In the emerging stages of writing, asking kindergartners to reflect—to make personal connections to a text and write about them—is difficult but, as Marty's story shows, worth the work. The first step is selecting books that will inspire children to make connections.

I introduce strategies separately and in this order: activating schema, creating mental images, questioning, and inferring, so I've set up this chapter that way. But in no way am I saying you'll turn into a pumpkin if you follow a different order of your own. For each, I select quality texts that illuminate the strategy, then model how to apply the strategy to enhance comprehension of the book. The book I choose the first day determines the subsequent readings. Choosing texts that connect similar threads strengthens comprehension about relationships, fostering continuity and flow of instruction. For example, if the strategy is creating mental images, I might choose *Grandfather's Trolley* (McMillan 1995), which illuminates the use of sound and movement words. My choice the next day might be *Shortcut* (Crews 1992) or *Night in the Country* (Rylant 1986) because the authors of both books use powerful sound and movement words to enrich their writing.

When introducing a strategy for the first time, I explain, "These are tools that good thinkers and readers use to understand what they are thinking and reading." I ask the children what tools, for example, a hairdresser would use. Quickly they answer scissors, combs, brushes. "Good thinkers and readers use tools as well," I tell them. With each thinking strategy we examine, I explain the purpose behind the strategy and how it helps readers understand what they read. I make a chart to summarize the strategies and serve as a reference:

> Good readers and thinkers use *tools* to help them understand what they have read. They
> * use their *schema* and make connections: they think about what they know and what it reminds them of
> * *visualize:* make pictures in their heads
> * *question:* ask questions when they don't understand or want to know more
> * *infer:* gather word and picture clues to figure out what is going on

Fifteen years ago I had more flexibility experimenting with all seven strategies. Now, however, my approach has changed, for reasons that will be all too familiar to every kindergarten teacher: more tests, added accountability, and the constantly rising standards that both keep us awake at night and keep us on our toes. So these days, I focus on the four strategies I have found to be most effective for kindergartners and address the other three (determining importance, synthesizing, and monitoring for meaning) informally, rather than give each its own six- to eight-week block. For example, when conferring with a child who's experienced a loss of words in trying to write a letter, I ask, "What's the most important thing you want to say, or ask, your mommy?" Or after reading a book about Martin Luther King Jr.'s life, I ask, "What's the most important thing Dr. King wanted us to remember?"

I model monitoring for meaning on a text level by periodically stopping and asking questions throughout a read-aloud and encouraging children to paraphrase the meaning. I address this strategy on a word level as well, when a child approaches an unknown word and comprehension breaks down. I model rereading, getting my mouth ready (matching the sound with the letters), inferring what a word means by looking at pictures, letter clues, and context, and then asking myself, "Does this make sense?"

The next sections provide a brief overview of how to introduce each of the four key strategies through a read-aloud and then how to apply each strategy to writing.

Activating Schema

When several of our classroom fish died, we followed our ritual, giving them a proper burial beneath the boughs of our evergreen trees. Numerous discussions surfaced about death and dying, leading to a reading of *Lifetimes*, by Bryan Melloine and Robert Ingpen (1983), *The Dead Bird*, by Margaret Wise Brown (1965), and *Nana Upstairs and Nana Downstairs* (dePaola 1973).

When modeling activating schema, be sure to choose texts you can connect to yourself. Before, during, and after the read-aloud, demonstrate how activating your background knowledge and recalling your own experiences aids comprehension. While reading, I suggest that children think about what the story reminds them of, what experiences in their lives the story connects to, and then think about how those memories might help them better understand the story.

So, for example, I shared with the group that *Nana Upstairs and Nana Downstairs* reminded me of several experiences involving my two grandmothers. I remember their visits on separate occasions and the special experiences I had with them, such as playing cards and beauty parlor. Grandma Fish would fall asleep and snore in the living room chair as the late afternoon sun filtered through the windows, while I brushed her fine, silver-gray hair and rolled it in pink plastic rollers. Many years later, when her health deteriorated, she came to live with us. Eventually, she lost her ability to walk and needed a wheelchair—something I thought of when, in the book, Tomie ties his grandmother to the back of the wheelchair so she doesn't flop out.

Near the end of the book, Tomie races to say hello to Nana Upstairs as part of his after-school ritual, only to find her bed empty, with a smooth bedspread and fluffed-up pillows. This scene brought me instantly back to Grandma Laura and my first experience with death. I can remember as if it were yesterday the empty feeling when I ran into the bedroom of her Brooklyn apartment and stared at the maroon cotton bedspread on her neatly made bed. This was my first experience with loss; I understood instantly that she would never come back.

In modeling comprehension strategies, I intersperse read-alouds with modeled writing. A few days after we first read *Nana Upstairs and Nana Downstairs*, I modeled writing a simple story about the memory of playing beauty parlor with my grandmother. As I retold my experience, I shared with the children the special feelings I had spending time with her alone, brushing her silver-gray hair. Because of my experiences with my grandma, I knew what it was like for Tomie to sit with Nana Upstairs and eat delectable sweets out of her candy box or just to sit and talk.

For Ceeci, *Nana Upstairs and Nana Downstairs* brought back fond memories of her great-great-grandma, whom she knew mostly through the many stories her father told. When her 106-year-old great-great-grandmother died in Mississippi, Ceeci and her dad traveled two long days to say good-bye. Ceeci drew a picture that showed herself and her dad driving. To the right was a figure of her grandma lying down, engulfed in a heart-shaped casket. "I WNT to Se My GRNMI IN hR KASKT" (*I went to see my grandma in her casket*), Ceeci wrote.

For many of my kindergartners, listening thoughtfully to text, questioning, and self-reflecting are novel experiences. So after finishing a read-aloud and connecting my experiences to the book, I encourage children to model what I have done and share their own experiences. For Ceeci, this connection was direct. At writing time, she immediately picked up her crayon and began drawing her last memory of her great-great-grandmother. Sometimes children are quiet, and I might say, "You may not be reminded of anything in *Nana Upstairs and Nana Downstairs* in the moment. But later on, something might take you back to the story, and you may want to talk or write about it then. . . . Let me know what you're thinking about, whenever it happens, so I can help you share your story with others."

In the first few months of school, when the writing experience is new, few students are ready to directly apply what they know and are reminded of from a read-aloud to their writing. So although a few children will write clearly about their connection to a text (Ceeci in the moment and Marty at a later date), I know that for most, the way they apply activating schema as a comprehension strategy will be to write what they know and care about, whether or not the subject connects to what we've just read. Children typically respond orally to a book and make their connections that way. It takes repeated exposure to the idea of linking experiences to text before most children can make that bridge in their writing.

So, for example, before sending children to their tables, I explain, "Tomie dePaola wrote about something he knew and cared a lot about; these were precious memories of his grandmas." I encourage the children to think and write about what the story reminded them of—or, if not that, to write about something they know and care about. All the time I spend listening to them helps me know what to suggest. "For example," I say, "I know that Francisco knows a lot about kitty cats. Anayansi knows a lot about doggies because she has Bello. Noehlie knows a lot about having older sisters and brothers. Think about what you know and care about, and write about it."

Most of the books I choose for read-alouds during our weeks of studying this strategy also encourage access to the emotional domain. The subjects of these books—a loved one dying, an experience of being bullied, a time you were really angry, the excitement of your own hiding place—instantly engage children. Most five-year-olds have direct access to emotion, making the connection to the text more engaging. It's easy to lose the students' interest if I choose, say, a book about the ocean and expect a group of city kids to understand and make connections to the sounds, textures, and experiences of the beach.

As the year progresses and children's schema and writing experience both broaden, they begin to write about memories that connect more directly to our reading. Even when we're focusing on a different comprehension strategy, I look for occasions to revisit learning from earlier in the year, giving children more chances to express new learning orally or through writing. For example, a child may experience being bullied on the playground, or in the lunchroom, six months into the year. I reread *Bailey the Big Bully* (Boyd 1989) if time allows, or revisit and summarize the text as we read the pictures together, eliciting memories and feelings. I encourage them to write, or share, memories in the moment, accessing the emotional and creative domains.

Capitalizing on teachable moments and asking the right questions at the right time will draw out a child's experience, enhance learning, and reveal new levels of comprehension.

Many times children will choose a book I've read aloud, bring it to their writing table, and fondly flip through the pages. When I see that happening, as I did with Marty, I know that something in the story has intrigued them, and I encourage them to record this new learning. The more experience children have with writing, the more willing they are to write about what they know. Even when this writing turns out not to make a personal connection to our reading, it's important to encourage children to write when they're inspired, to help them learn in the creative and emotional domains.

One mid-January day when we were in the midst of studying the civil rights movement, I read *This Is the Dream* (Shore and Alexander 2006) to the class. Later that morning, I could tell that Anayansi was struck with this movement as she took the book to her table and stared at the illustration of hundreds of black people marching in line, holding signs. I knelt beside her and asked, "Do you remember why the black people are marching?"

"To change the laws. . . . They don't have the same rights."

"That's right. Many years ago, black people didn't have the same rights as white people. Do you remember what you call this march?"

Anayansi responded, "A protest." I could tell she was deeply moved by this march. Twenty-five years of working with five-year-olds has shown me repeatedly how compassionate they are about everything from the dead chick that didn't develop in the incubator to grand issues such as the civil rights movement. Anayansi's compassion led her to a deeper understanding of the struggles black people went through during this period. (See Figure 7–2.)

Sometimes sharing with the group on the oval becomes the catalyst for connecting discoveries to writing. Abdili, for example, told the class how he'd discovered that jaguars and leopards have different markings on their fur: the rosettes on a jaguar have a black dot in the center, while the leopard's rosettes are empty. Sharing this discovery inspired him to record it in his writing. He did this through a detailed illustration with labels, reinforcing the power of visuals in representing schema. This was a simple yet powerful way of sharing new information for a second language learner with limited language skills. (See Figure 7–3.)

Creating Mental Images

THE BIG RED BALL

"We've talked a lot about how readers use their schema to understand what they are thinking and reading. You guys do it all the time when you tell me what you know before I share a book. When you're reading *Zoobooks* magazines or nonfiction books, you think about what you know, and you make sense of the photograph or illustration. Well, schema is just one tool that great thinkers and readers use. Today we're going to talk about another tool called *visualizing*. Can you guys say that?"

The children echo my words, and I continue. "*Visualize* is a rich word that means 'to make a picture in your head.' The way a great writer helps you, the readers, make

FIGURE 7–2 *Anayansi's response to* This Is the Dream: The black people are marching to change the laws! This is called a protest!

FIGURE 7–3 *Abdili's text and drawings, with rosettes labeled:* Jaguar. Leopard.

those pictures is by using rich words. Authors carefully choose interesting words because they want their stories to come alive." I have found that the word *visualizing* is easier for kindergartners to comprehend than the more common term *mental images*, which I use when explaining the strategy to visiting teachers or parents.

Adding a single word to a story can bring their writing to life, I tell the kids. "For example, close your eyes and picture a ball. Now picture a *red* ball. Now picture a *big* red ball. Now picture a big red *bouncing* ball!" Children's heads bounce in time with the image. Tana Hoban's *A Children's Zoo* (1985) is a great follow-up text for demonstrating this point. "Black, white, waddles . . . Penguin. Black and white, striped, gallops . . . Zebra. Strong, shaggy, roars . . . Lion."

Another example: "I have a beautiful book to share with you today called *Salt Hands* [Aragon 1989]. I want you to listen carefully to the rich words that Jane Chelsea Aragon uses. She chose her words with great care so that you would feel like you were right there in the story with this little girl. You'll have a chance to hear this book again tomorrow, and we'll talk about the rich words then. For now, I just want you to listen."

The next day, as I read the book again, I stop and reread selected passages, describing the richness and contrasting it with simple, plain language. "In the night I woke up. I heard a rustle or a breath." As I read the word *rustle*, I wriggle my fingers in a tub full of dry leaves we collected in the fall, making a crinkling sound. "Jane Chelsea Aragon didn't just say, 'I heard something.' She said, 'I heard a rustle or a breath.'"

Further on in the text, I stop and contrast how the author described the little girl getting salt. "She didn't just say the girl went in and dumped salt into her hands. She said, 'Quietly I went in and sprinkled some salt into my hands.' Her choice of words made me feel like I was right there in the story. I could see her quietly tiptoeing inside her house and carefully sprinkling a small amount of salt in her hands." After finishing the read-aloud, I say, "Today in your writing, before you pick up your pencil or crayon, I want you to close your eyes and picture what you are writing about. See the detail and color; add this richness to your illustration and words."

After several weeks of firmly grounding the notion of rich language, I help the children divide these words into sensory categories. "Many of the rich words you notice can be put into groups. For example, some words we can *see*. Those are called *visual words*. Can you say that?" The children echo my words. "Remember in *Green Eyes*, A. Birnbaum [1981] described Green Eyes' box as 'a big wide box with four high walls.'" As I echo Birnbaum's words, my hands simultaneously spread apart, eliciting *wide* from the children, and then stretch above and below, eliciting *high*. "Because the writer used those words, we could *see* that box. And remember the way he described her blanket? A ssso . . ."

"A soft pink blanket," the children chime in.

"Yes, great remembering! Well, *soft* is a word we can . . ." I rub my fingers together. "Feel!" they exclaim.

"Yes! You guys are so smart! Words we can feel are called *touch words.* Remember how Tyrus described the rock he found a while ago? He didn't say 'I found a rock.' He said, 'I found a . . .'"

The children enthusiastically finish the description: "A smooth, round stone shaped like a juggling ball!"

"*Smooth* is a great touch word. *Round stone shaped like a juggling ball* are wonderful visual words. Not only can we see his stone, but we can feel it as well!

"So writers use visual words and touch words, and many of the books we've read have *sound* words, too. In *Shortcut,* Donald Crews [1992] included the sound of the train throughout the story, making it louder as the train neared us: 'Whoo-whoo-*whoo-whoo-whoo*!' Marty did that too, when he wrote about his dogs Angel and Killer. Remember the sound he included in Killer's talking bubble?"

All the children immediately make a snarling face, baring menacing teeth as they growl, "Rrrrrrr!"

"Bruce McMillan used many sound words and *movement* words in *Grandfather's Trolley* [1995]. Sounds words are words we hear, and movement words are words we can act out." I pick up *Grandfather's Trolley* from our read-aloud tub, which sits beside my chair, and reread a descriptive passage while I simultaneously play a sound bite I recorded on a CD of a moving trolley. Swaying from side to side, experiencing the rickety, bumpy ride, I lean back and squint, keeping the breeze out of my eyes just like the little girl in the text: "The trolley swayed from side to side. Clackety-clackety, clackety-clack. I rocked with the car from side to side. Clackety-clackety, clackety-clack." After reading this passage, I share with the children, "Bruce McMillan purposely chose these sound and movement words because he wanted us to hear and feel the movement of the trolley."

This process continues over several weeks, as I clearly define other sensory categories, such as taste and smell words. I chart these words as children identify them in context, elevating authors and children side by side (see Figure 7–4). "Kasmira, I loved how you described your new pants. You didn't just say, 'I have new pants.' You used great visual words, touch words, and sound words. 'I have new purple corduroy pants! They go, "Whoosh! Whoosh!"' It's just like A. Birbaum did in *Green Eyes* and Bruce McMillan did in *Grandfather's Trolley.*" (See Figure 7–5.)

The top of the chart states, "Rich Words—words that paint a picture for the reader." Under this title, I label categories on consecutive sheets of chart paper and list words the children have written, as well as words chosen from selected read-alouds. For example, I listed Kasmira's *Whoosh! Whoosh!* under "Sound" and listed *sprinkled* (from Aragon's *Salt Hands* [1989]) under "Movement."

FIGURE 7–4 *I model writing as I add words to our rich language chart.*

FIGURE 7–5 *Kasmira's sensory-rich writing:* I have new purple corduroy pants! They go, "Whoosh! Whoosh!"

Visual: words you see
Sound: words you hear
Movement: words you can move to
Taste: words you taste
Touch: words you feel
Smell: words you smell

WHAT WE CAN LEARN

Hearing rich language in read-alouds lays the groundwork that allows students' thinking and writing to happen. It's important to read a text in its entirety, allowing an author's words to stand alone. Only after children have heard a text read uninterrupted and gained familiarity with it are they able to reflect and examine an author's style.

When introducing the strategy of creating mental images to kindergartners, it's important (as it is with any strategy) to be as simple and clear as possible. For example, the dictionary definition of *visualize* is "to form a mental image or vision." I define it as "to make a picture in your head" because that's easier for kindergartners to understand.

In the first few weeks, applying this strategy to writing is simple: everyone tries to use rich words that paint a picture for the reader. I don't distinguish the different senses connected to different words until I'm sure that the children fully comprehend the notion of visualizing. Many of my students enter kindergarten unable to identify the five senses, let alone use them to put words into categories, so it would only confuse them if we started that way.

I firmly ground children in identifying rich words. Then, a few weeks later, I set a new challenge by asking them to define *categories* of sensory words. As children gain deeper understanding of sensory words, my language becomes more precise as I send them to write. I specifically encourage them to use visual words, sound words, touch, smell, taste, and movement words.

Real props, such as leaves for making a rustling sound or a recorded sound bite of a trolley, appeal directly to the senses and thus enhance comprehension. Sounds can also help children understand something far removed from their own experience, for example, the sounds of birds chirping in a rain forest or the gentle sounds of waves lapping on the shore.

Several weeks later, however, revisiting read-alouds or a child's writing and identifying which words evoke, say, sound or movement starts to make sense. For example, with *Salt Hands* (Aragon 1989), I ask the children what kind of word *sprinkled* is. "Is *sprinkled* a word we taste? Is it a word we smell or feel? Is it a word we see?"

To that last question, the children chime in, "Yeah!"

"Good thinking! Can we also *move* to it? Show me *sprinkle*." When they do, I point out that many words can fit into more than one category. "So where do you think we should put the word *sprinkled* on our chart? Is it mainly a word we see, like *striped* and *polka dot*, or is mainly a word we can move to and act out?"

They unanimously agree: "It's a movement word."

"Great! Let's put it under movement words." Already the children understand that there's no single right way to categorize words; it all depends on the context.

APPLYING MENTAL IMAGES TO ILLUSTRATIONS AND MODELED WRITING

For a kindergartner, illustrations carry the same weight as language. It's important to maintain that connection by continually emphasizing the role that color and detail play to enhance the meaning of stories. Gina's illustration of her loose tooth from Chapter 6 (see Figure 6–3) is a beautiful example; I feel as if I'm inside her mouth experiencing the rocking motion of her tooth. *My tooth is wiggly and moves forward and back!* Her words are rich, and the illustration says it all.

Barbara Berger's *Grandfather Twilight* (1984) is a powerful example of this same phenomenon, creating mental images with detailed illustrations and just a few words. Her ethereal drawings of Grandfather walking through the woods, with the clouds dragging behind, draw you into the story by tapping into not just the sense of sight but those of touch, sound, and movement as well. Detailed illustrations tell a story just like rich words.

Sometimes I revisit a piece of writing as another way of applying mental images as a comprehension strategy. For example, the children experience this repetition when I redraw the picture of playing beauty parlor with Grandma Fish. This time I use rich, descriptive words to express the light coming through the window, her appearance as she dozed, and the pink plastic rollers I used to put into her hair. I break this modeled piece of writing into two days, adding detail to the illustration and lengthening my writing. I purposefully model revisions, for instance, by crossing out the exclamation point and demonstrating how to add on (see Figure 7–6).

This time, before releasing children to their writing tables, I add detail to the instructions I've given before: "Today in your writing, I want you to close your eyes and picture your story. Ask yourself, 'What does it look like; what does it feel like; what does it taste like; what does it sound like; or what does it smell like?' Think of using visual words, touch words, taste words, sound words, smell words, and move-ment words if you can. Don't forget to add richness to your illustrations as well. Add lots of color and detail; make us feel like we are right there in your story."

The following two stories show how to incorporate the strategy, *creating mental images*, in the contexts of sharing, community, and outdoor play.

As the late afternoon sun filtered through the window, Grandma Fish dozed off in the living room chair! I brushed her silver gray hair and rolled pink plastic rollers into her fine hair.

FIGURE 7–6 *Modeled writing of my experience with Grandma Fish*

CHEETOS

Anayansi walked into the classroom one morning, her lips lined with reddish-orange crumbs. "Sweetie, have you been eating Cheetos?" A big grin spread across her face as she nodded; she was obviously excited about having these delectables in her backpack. It was a golden opportunity to develop language and explore mental images more deeply in the contexts of literacy, sharing, and community. As we shared on the oval, I said playfully, "Anayansi, tell us what the Cheetos tasted like. Try to use rich words to describe them."

Because we'd been working on using sensory language, the words *hot* and *spicy* instantly flew from her mouth. "I love that description!" I told her. "Hot, spicy Cheetos! Wow! I feel like my mouth is on fire," I said as I pretended to fan my tongue. "What do they sound like as you bite into them?"

She took a moment and then blurted out, "Crunchy!"

"I love it! Hot, spicy, crunchy Cheetos! That's awesome, Anayansi! Not only can I feel the fire in my mouth, but I can hear my teeth as they crunch into them!"

WHAT WE CAN LEARN

I incorporate strategy instruction throughout the day and in different contexts of learning. Anayansi's experience was brought forth in the context of sharing and community. Because this inquiry happened in the group, all the children got to benefit from the language I elicited from her. I was intentionally listening and asking questions about words, thus generating a context of literacy and highlighting the strategy, *creating mental images.* Even though she chose not to write about the Cheetos, I frequently referenced Anayansi's precise choice of language. "Remember the taste and sound words Anayansi used to describe those yummy snacks that made her lips orangey-red?"

The *Hh* sound would be all the prompting the kids needed before chiming in, "Hot, spicy, crunchy Cheetos!" The children used these words all year long, as if they were theirs as well.

Before releasing the children to their tables, I would say, "In your writing today, think about Anayansi. Use taste words, words we can taste; sound words, words we hear; visual words, words we see; or movement words, words we can act out. Make us feel like we are right there in your story!"

BORROWING LANGUAGE

As Tajanee arrived late for school one Monday in November, I was struck by the sound of the black lacquered beads dangling from the ends of her beautiful, tightly woven braids. All eyes were riveted on Tajanee as she sat down on the oval for the remainder of our morning share. It was a perfect moment to reinforce the importance of sound and movement words.

"My gosh, Tajanee, what *gorgeous* beads you have," I said. "I *love* the sound!"

"Thanks," she said modestly.

"Guys, do you realize I *heard* Tajanee come into the class *before* I saw her?" Then I turned to Tajanee. "Sweetheart, go back to the door and pretend you're just walking in." She smiled with anticipation and jumped to her feet.

Whispering, I said to the rest of the children, "Close your eyes and be quiet; I want you just to *listen*." The children's eyes squeezed tightly with effort as their faces scrunched, listening one more time to the rhythmic clatter of the hair beads.

"Tajanee, how could you describe this incredible sound?"

She shrugged her shoulders and gently shook her head. "I don't know."

"What were your beads *doing*, honey?"

"They were shakin'!"

"Like what?" I asked.

"Like dancin'!"

"Wow! I love it! 'My beads were shakin' like dancin'!'" I proudly stated, echoing her words. "You've got to write that down! I'll help you during writing, OK?"

We exchanged huge smiles. I had planted a seed for writing, and she was thrilled with the suggestion. Later that morning during writing workshop, I helped Tajanee sound out this beautiful description of her beads and continued to probe for movement and sound words. But when her beads weren't moving, she remained as silent as they did.

We ended writing for the morning and headed out to the playground for recess. Hannah stood watching Tajanee jump rope and listened carefully to the conversation I was having with her. "Tajanee, I love the way you described your beads: 'My beads were shakin' like dancin'.' That's *beautiful*! Can you think of any great *sound* words you could add to describe them?"

She was quiet.

"Sweetheart, stop jumping for a moment. Close your eyes, swing your head from side to side, and *listen* to them. What do you *hear*?"

Hannah burst out, "Clickety-click!"

"Wow, Hannah! Those are *great* sound words! Tajanee, you might want to borrow those words for your writing. What do you think?" I left the question unanswered.

The next morning, with support, Tajanee added Hannah's "borrowed" descriptive words to her writing. Kasmira, Tajanee's writing buddy, sat nearby and listened attentively as I reread what Tajanee had written: "My beads were shakin' like dancin'. Clickety-click." I'm careful always to read students' writing aloud because the sound and the distance often help them gain clarity.

"Is there anything you might want to add?" I carefully prompted. I wanted to make sure that Tajanee had completed her thoughts.

Kasmira chimed in, "Shakety-shake," as if *she* owned those words.

"Wow! What do you think, Tajanee? Want to add those great sound and movement words?"

Tajanee beamed, agreeing they were a perfect adjunct to her story. "MY BEDS WR SHAKN LIK DASN! KLTE KLK! SHAKDE SHAK!" (*My beads were shakin' like dancin'! Clickety-click! Shakety-shake!*)

Listening carefully to a child, taking her lead, and asking specific questions that tap the senses are the keys to eliciting language when teaching mental images as a comprehension strategy. Anayansi's, Kasmira's, and Tajanee's stories show how a teacher can help develop rich language in the contexts of sharing, community, and literacy. When Kasmira walked to the oval first thing in the morning wearing her new corduroy pants, I noticed the great sound they made. This prompted a wonderful discussion of the power of sounds. Out of Kasmira's mouth came the words "Whoosh! Whoosh!" I encouraged her to record those words in her writing.

With Tajanee, we started in the context of literacy and shifted the lens when we went outside to play. That shift, from literacy to play, pulled forth rich language when the sound and movement of her beads elicited the words *clickety-click* from her friend Hannah. While Anayansi came up with her descriptions of Cheetos only orally, Kasmira and Tajanee recorded their descriptive passages in their daybooks, returning them to the context of literacy. When children lack the language to express their thoughts completely, they'll often use another child's words to help communicate. Borrowing language, as Tajanee did with Hannah's *clickety-click*, is not plagiarism; it's a way of learning from one another.

In teaching mental images, I want children to experiment with the use of rich language, both orally and on paper. I evaluate their progress by listening to their talk and the comments they make about an author's choice of words during a read-aloud and by the language they use in their writing.

Questioning

Questioning is the foundation of all good thinking and learning. It's the most productive of all the comprehension strategies because it pushes us to deepen our thinking and our engagement with life, thus broadening our learning. I use questions to clarify children's thinking and to teach comprehension. Of course, questions can also *test* comprehension, but in my classroom this is not their primary use.

Developmentally, kindergartners are just beginning to determine what constitutes a question. Early in the year when I ask, "Who has a question?" most children respond by making statements. So I use the term *wonder*—"What are you wondering about?"—to bring into the open the questions that form in their minds. The more we wonder, the more we learn; the more we learn, the more we wonder, a never-ending active cycle of growth, which Rabbit teaches us so beautifully in *Why Is the Sky Blue?* (Grindley 1996).

After reading *Why Is the Sky Blue?* Abdili asked: "WidO LAdEbGS HAAV A LOT F NMBRS?" (*Why do ladybugs have a lot of numbers?*). This was his way of asking why

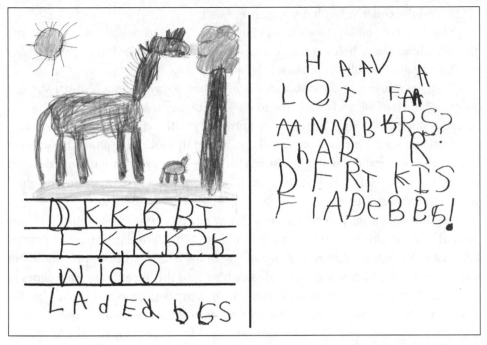

FIGURE 7–7 *Abdili's wondering:* Why do ladybugs have a lot of numbers? There are different kinds of ladybugs!

different ladybugs have different numbers of spots. The question came from looking closely at ladybugs in the books he was reading, mirroring the same process Rabbit taught us: that our questions frequently come from close observation. Since the class took an interest in his wondering, I read books on ladybugs and discovered that there are numerous varieties, which have different-colored spots (Some are orange with white dots!) and have between two and sixteen spots. He incorporated this new learning in his writing the following day (see Figure 7–7). When children have a purpose for their wondering, they come up with questions that stretch their own thinking. Remember, it's the *process* of asking questions that matters and further pushes our engagement with the world, not the answers.

ROSIE THE TARANTULA

As we begin our oval share one day, I say, "Good morning, guys. I need to share something really cool Sheldon and I noticed this morning. Sheldon, tell everyone what we saw."

"Rosie has web," he responds.

I gently support him by saying, "Sheldon, a web is what spiders make. The white stuff that comes out of the back of their abdomen is called . . ."

He and the children finish my sentence: "Silk!"

"Sheldon, can you say, 'Rosie let out lots of silk!'?" He echoes my words. "Yes, and this silk comes out of holes in the bottom of her abdomen, called *sss* . . ."

Once again, they fill in the blank: "Spinnerets!"

"Guys, as Sheldon and I looked into Rosie's tank today, we noticed that she had let out a bunch of silk and attached it to the sides of the tank." Then I model the idea of questioning by asking, "Does anyone know why?" The children are silent.

"Sheldon, quick, get Rosie's journal and record this great question." We support Sheldon as he stretches out his curiosity in the journal we keep for our tarantula. "WI IS rose LtIng OUt SLK?" (*Why is Rosie letting out silk?*). After Sheldon writes the question, Jenecia illustrates it.

I use this opportunity to model what I know, the process of questioning, and how I might find the answer. I share with the children, "This is confusing to me. Tarantulas usually let out, or discharge, a bed of silk in a small area before they molt, but Rosie has scattered her silk all around, attaching it to the log and the glass panes of the tank. Even though her silk is all over the tank, my best guess is that she's getting ready to molt just like Houdinni. I'll need to do some more reading, or talk to an expert on tarantulas, to find out for sure. Meanwhile, we're going to have to observe her really closely." The children know about molting from our garter snake, but I haven't made this connection to spiders prior to today.

The following day on the oval, all twenty-two children reenact the molting process through movement. They get down on all fours, spinning round and round in circles, discharging silk from their spinnerets and carefully listening to the beat of my drum as I describe the molting process. "You are no longer a little girl or little boy; you are a spider with four legs on one side and . . . how many on the other? You have how many legs altogether?" I purposefully leave blanks in my description or ask questions to engage the children. "You have eight eyes and two body parts, a cephalothorax—remember, that's your head and thorax crunched together—and an . . . what?" "Abdomen!" "Right now, your skin is beginning to feel *really* tight. You have stopped eating and stopped moving. Something inside you is changing; your exoskeleton is beginning to split." Within moments, they rest on their backs on top of a soft bed of silk with their legs in the air, slowly wiggling out of their exoskeleton. Lorraine volunteers to record this thinking in the journal: "I thic rose is GoinG to MOLt!" (*I think Rosie is going to molt!*).

Two weeks later, Rosie flips onto her back, beginning the molting process. The children and I watch this miraculous transformation intermittently all morning long. In Rosie's journal the children first record, "ROSe MAD A BED OF SLK! She FlPt OVr on hr Bak!" Later they add, "Then She MOTltlt!" (*Rosie made a bed of silk! She flipped over on her back! Then she molted!*)

QUESTIONING ON THE OVAL

We're in our third week of exploring questioning as a comprehension strategy, and questions are blossoming everywhere. Amiaja (*MY-A-sha*) wonders why baby elephants have red hair. Jenecia wonders why she doesn't live with her brothers. Haley wonders if our snail is a girl or a boy. Ruben misses his father and wonders whether he will ever leave Chihuahua and return to Denver.

Good readers ask questions before, during, and after reading, I tell the children, in order to understand what they have read. I continue modeling my own thinking in a variety of contexts (sharing, community, literacy) while encouraging children to express theirs. When genuine questions surface, I always respond and plant a seed: "What a great wondering question! You might want to write about that." Many of the children take my lead.

After I've modeled wondering through a read-aloud, a few children record in their daybooks questions that actually connect to the text. The majority, however, continue writing about whatever personal questions interest them. That's OK; I don't expect everyone to be asking questions that connect to the text all the time. Once children are generating and recording meaningful questions for themselves, I suggest they reflect and write their best answer to a question on the back of the page. The purpose is to promote critical reasoning. If a child has no idea how to respond and is seeking an answer, I bring it up for discussion with the class, capitalizing on the context. Other times, I support children individually in conducting research.

The children's writing samples in Figures 7–8 and 7–9 show the questions that interested these young writers and their responses. Writing random questions that interest them is just as useful as writing questions specifically connected to text I've read aloud because children are at the helm of their own learning.

THE OTHER SIDE

After spending time building schema about the civil rights movement, I introduce the book *The Other Side*, by Jacqueline Woodson (2001). "I have a beautiful book to share. It will make you think and ask lots of questions. Today, I'm just going to read it so we can enjoy the book the way the author wanted us to. Tomorrow, when I reread it, you're going to have a chance to peek inside my head and listen to my thoughts and the questions I have as a reader. I'll need you to be quiet and just listen. Save your thinking until the next day when I read the book once again. You'll get to share your thoughts and questions then."

On the inside jacket of *The Other Side*, the book is described as "a moving, lyrical narrative told in the hopeful voice of a child confused about the fence someone has built in her yard and racial tension that divides her world." Table 7–1 shows some

FIGURE 7–8 *One child's question:* When did T-rex sleep? On my CD I heard it say he hunted night and day! I think T-rex sleepwalked!

FIGURE 7–9 *Another student's question:* Why don't my brothers live with me? My brothers have different moms and dads.

of the questions I share with the children as we read and reread the book over two days. The questions on the third day are designed to clarify thinking and deepen comprehension.

I can tell the children are deeply moved with this book by their animated and engaged responses. After we finish the story, I prompt them to respond by writing any questions they have or ideas they're particularly struck with. As usual, many of the questions they write don't relate to the book, so I ask my own questions to get them going. Marty and Cesar are working collaboratively when I ask them, "Why do you think the book is called *The Other Side*?"

Marty's written response: "I tHK it MENS HAf AND HAf!" (*I think it means half and half!*).

"Tell me what you mean by that, Marty."

"The black people live on this side and white people live on the other." As he delivers this explanation, his hands move, delineating the two sides of the fence.

"Wow, that's awesome thinking! What do you think Annie and Clover wanted?"

The two boys write, "THA WNt THE FNS NOKT DON SO THA KOD Be TOGTHR FOrVr!" (*They wanted the fence knocked down so they could be together forever!*).

I encourage Marty and Cesar to close their eyes and visualize what this might look like before drawing. I ask, "What would it look like if that happened? What might the girls be doing?" They beautifully illustrate a tire swing hanging from a backyard tree and two friends smiling, flying kites.

Meanwhile, in response to the text, Kasmira independently writes, "Why ARe PeAPOLe BROWn BLAcK AND WhIte?" (*Why are people brown, black, and white?*). Looking over her shoulder, I notice she has already begun to answer her question on the back: "I ThInK GOD DRAWeD US On A Pece OF PAPeR." (*I think God drew us on a piece of paper.*). I can't help but interject and ask, "And then what?" I leave to confer with other children and return later to read her response: "AND ThReW US On enRTh." (*and threw us on Earth.*). I'm moved by the depth of her words. (See Figure 7–10.)

The next day I ask the group, "Why do you think the author wrote this story? Remember, lots of times authors write books and songs for a reason. What do you think Jacqueline Woodson wanted you to remember?"

"About Martin Luther King!" they respond.

"And what did *he* want us to remember?"

"That everybody has the same rights!"

"And what else?" I ask.

"We should love one another!"

"What does that mean for Annie and Clover?"

"So they can play together and be friends forever!"

TABLE 7–1 *Questions About* The Other Side	
Day 2 Modeling	
My Questions	**My Self-Reflective Responses**
What does "the other side" mean?	I'm not sure.
I wonder why Mama said not to climb over the fence when you play. Why wasn't it safe?	Was it broken?
Why did she stare [pointing to the white girl] and never sit on the fence with anybody?	Maybe she was shy.
I wonder what her [black girl's] mother meant by "Because that's the way things have always been."	I don't understand, so I'm just going to read on.
I wonder why the little girl [pointing to the white girl] looked sad when she [black girl] saw her in town.	Maybe she wanted to play with her. It looks like their mamas are walking in different directions.
I wonder why their mamas say they shouldn't go to the other side.	Maybe the girls don't like one another, so their moms don't want them playing together.
Why didn't Clover's mom tell her to get down off the fence? I wonder what Annie meant by "Someday somebody's going to come along and knock this old fence down." I wonder what knocking down the fence would look like.	Maybe she thought Clover wasn't bothering her.

TABLE 7–1 *Questions About* The Other Side	
Day 3 Engagement	
My Questions to Stimulate Children's Responses	**Children's Responses**
What do you think "the other side" means?	Black people live on one side and white people on the other.
Why did Mama say not to climb over the fence when you play?	It was broken. She didn't want nobody to get hurt.
Why do you think she just stared and never sat on the fence with anybody?	'Cause her mama told her not to.
What do you think she meant by "Because that's the way things have always been?"	(No response.)
Look closely at the illustration and how Annie and Clover are dressed. Do you think this story is taking place now, or a long time ago?	A long time ago!
How do you know?	'Cause they're wearing long dresses and hats.
Think back to a time when people weren't treated the same. . . .	That's like Martin Luther King; they didn't have the same rights. . . .
Why do you think she looked sad?	'Cause she couldn't play with her.
But why couldn't they play together?	'Cause one was black and one was white.
Why do you think their mamas said they shouldn't go to the other side?	Their mamas didn't want them playing together 'cause she was white and she was black!
Why didn't Clover's mom tell her to get down off the fence?	'Cause she wasn't doing nothing to that girl.
What did Annie mean by "Someday somebody's going to come along and knock this old fence down?"	(No response.)
What did Annie want?	The fence knocked down.
But why?	So they could play together!
What would it look like if that fence were knocked down?	They'd be friends! They'd be runnin' around playing hide and seek!
Why do you think the fence was put there?	To keep black people on one side and white people on the other!

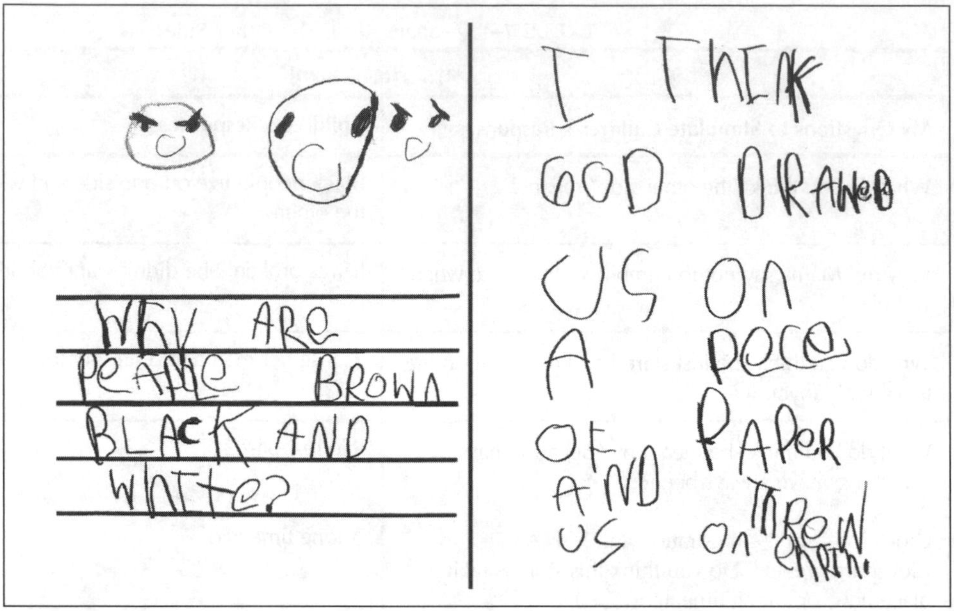

FIGURE 7–10 *Kasmira's powerful response to* The Other Side

Asking questions to individuals in the group, and supporting this process through inquiry, promotes new learning when everyone listens to the discussion and thinks about his own response.

WHAT WE CAN LEARN

The contexts of sharing, community, and literacy nurture rich thinking and questioning. Questions come first from my interactions with children and from following their lead. I ask different questions with different groups, both in read-alouds and in daily conversations. There's no all-purpose list of questions that works with all children in all circumstances, but certain methods and ways of thinking can get you started.

To begin, I follow four steps when using read-alouds to model questioning as a strategy:

- stopping and modeling questions that confuse me as a reader, making my thinking public (day two)
- modeling my best answers to those questions (day two)
- asking children the same questions, stimulating their responses (day three, during a reread)

- asking additional questions to clarify children's thinking, deepening comprehension (day three, during a reread)

When using *The Other Side*, I structure the read-aloud to direct children's thinking in how to comprehend the book, using the strategy *questioning*. I integrate my own questions and thoughts, asking children to hold onto their thinking until the third day.

Day two of the read-aloud is spent modeling questions. I'm selective about the responses to questions I model, not wanting to reveal too much or tamper with a child's interpretation and comprehension of the book. I want to model a reasonable response to the kinds of questions that are likely to surface. On day three we revisit these same questions, listening to children's responses and asking further questions to clarify their thinking and deepen comprehension. I use questioning as a tool to facilitate making sense throughout the text, not at the end to test comprehension. How children respond determines my next question, stimulating the process of inquiry.

It takes repeated modeling before most children can transfer their questions and thoughts to paper. I stress that many of our questions are generated through close observation, as Rabbit pointed out in *Why Is the Sky Blue?* (Grindley 1996). We talk about Alicia noticing the ants marching on a log in her aunt's backyard, Jane Goodall and her study of chimpanzees, and Sheldon's observation of Rosie and her silk. In each case, observation caused someone to stop, wonder, and search for answers.

After presenting a question, I ask the children for feedback. I always make the point that finding the answer isn't the most important part; it's the *process* of questioning that stretches our thinking. I brainstorm with children how I might find the answer if I need to, eliciting resources such as books, the Internet, movies, and experts in the field.

I'm constantly amazed at the way children ask questions specific to their personality, experience, and interests. Toneeshia, who was having trouble adjusting to the class (see Chapter 4), wanted to know "HOW KM PePL don't Gt aLOG?" (*How come people don't get along?*). On the back of her paper, she added, "tha Don't LIC Wne antHr." (*They don't like one another.*). And Tyrhon (*Ty-RON*), whom I had confronted about his untied shoelaces, wrote, "HoW DO YOR SHOLASZ KM NDN?" (*How do your shoelaces come undone?*). His answer: "I THK RNINg SoPR FAST MAKS YOR STRINg KM N DN!" (*I think running superfast makes your string come undone!*).

The two of them could not have picked better questions to ask; I'd been silently asking the same ones myself: "Why can't you get along with the other kids, Toneeshia? They're really trying to work with you! How can I help you become a kind friend? And Tyrhon, what *is* the deal with your shoelaces? How can those long bows unravel every single morning? What are you doing to them?"

After children have experience with generating questions, and understand the purpose for doing so, I use a read-aloud to model how we can answer our own questions. This is the language I use with the children:

- Go back and reread.
- Read on! Many times our questions are answered later in the book.
- Think about what you know; use your schema and think about what this reminds you of.
- Infer: listen to the word clues and look closely at the picture clues to figure out what's going on.
- Talk with a friend; ask a buddy what he thinks something means.
- If you're reading a nonfiction book, a book that is true, and your question is not answered, ask me for help in doing research.

To an observer, the process of questioning may be most apparent when a child sits in the author's chair and I ask questions to elicit detail and develop understanding of her experience. I continually prompt the children with "Tell me more." It's important to label the process in the moment: "If I had never asked these questions, I never would have known . . ."

So, for instance, when Gina reflected on *Grandfather Twilight* (Berger 1984) and wrote the following questions in her daybook, I knew she was recording the process of thinking, going deeper as she progressed, echoing the same steps I use with children in the author's chair. Her questions were independently generated.

- HOW DZ HE ThRO THE PRL IN THE SKI? (*How does he throw the pearl in the sky?*)
- DAD HE US MAJEK OR DAD HE JIST THRO AT N THE SKI? (*Did he use magic or did he just throw it in the sky?*)
- WI ASNT THAR AN ND to THEPRLS? (*Why isn't there an end to the pearls?*)

Her questions led to further wondering, continuing the process of inquiry for herself. Gina was particularly intrigued by her last question, so after her share in the author's chair, we opened this discussion to the class. It was another opportunity to use the "teachers" around us to talk about the never-ending cycle of the moon.

My goal in teaching questioning as a comprehension strategy is to model authentic questions, encourage children to ask questions to which they don't know the answers, and instill a sense of wonder. I want children using questioning to reason critically, answering the unknowns for themselves and enhancing comprehension. My expectation is for the majority of children to implement questioning across content areas. In writing, my goal is for some children to record questions directly related to the text and for most to record questions they personally wonder about. I evaluate this accomplishment by listening to their conversation and their comments during a read-aloud and by considering the questions they write.

Inferring

Although my students don't hear the word *inference* until later in the year, they're familiar with the concept right from the start. From the early weeks of school, I model how to infer with nonfiction and wordless books. So, for instance, when I present the wordless text *Good Dog, Carl* (Day 1997), I make my own thinking visible. "I see the baby sitting near an opening, and it looks like there's a basket full of clothes nearby," I say as I examine one of the pictures at the beginning of the book. "Wait a minute, above the opening there's a sign that says 'Laundry.'" I point and run my finger underneath the word. "I think it might be a laundry chute." I explain the word *chute* and its function.

Then, when looking at the next page, I say, "Carl's running downstairs. I bet he's trying to catch the baby!" As I turn the page, we see the baby sitting with clothes beside him, looking up and waving to Carl, who's standing in the open doorway. I use questioning to help children critically reason and infer for themselves where the baby is.

"Where's the baby? Where do you think he landed?" I ask.

"Downstairs!" they reply.

"How do you know?"

"Carl is up there."

"Where?"

"At the top!"

"Of what?"

"The stairs."

"And where is the baby?"

"Down there!"

"Yes, what do you call downstairs?" I prompt them with "*Ba . . .*"

The children fill in the missing word: "Basement!"

"What do you see near the baby in the basement? Look closely."

"Clothes!"

"Yes, the baby ended up downstairs in the basement with the dirty clothes. Great thinking!"

Later, when it's time to introduce the six- to eight-week block in which we'll formally look at inference, I do more explaining: "Many times an author doesn't come right out and tell you what's going on. As a reader, you've got to infer. *Infer* is rich word that means 'to gather clues to figure out what's happening.' As a reader, you look for the word clues that an author leaves or the picture clues that an illustrator leaves. They leave those clues to make their stories more interesting and because they want you to *think*.

"*Infer* might be a new word, but you guys do it all the time when you read pictures in *Zoobooks* magazines. The other day when Haley shared on the oval that the goose was protecting her goslings from a cat, she was inferring. What she saw in the picture was the goose's neck stretched out long, with its bill opened wide. The goslings were behind the mother, and there was a hunched-up cat with its hair standing on end. Haley looked carefully at all those things in the picture, and she *inferred* that the cat was trying to attack the baby geese.

"Anayansi did the same thing when she shared coming home to her house and finding garbage dumped everywhere. She didn't *see* Bello push the trash can and pull garbage out. She inferred this. By looking at the clues in her house—the garbage can tipped over, trash on the kitchen floor, doggie prints, and no one else at home—she inferred that Bello was responsible for the mess!"

THIS QUIET LADY

"Today I'm going to read you a special book called *This Quiet Lady*, by Charlotte Zolotow [1992]. It's a short story, so first I want you just to listen. Then I'll reread it and share my thinking; save yours until tomorrow when I reread the book once again. I want you to pay close attention to the word clues, and particularly the picture clues, that the writer and illustrator left to help you figure out what the story is all about. You're going to have to infer."

This Quiet Lady is a simple yet sophisticated book in which a little girl uses framed photographs and a photo album to tell the story of her mother, from her mother's birth to the girl's own birth. But the writer never directly says who this little girl is or how she is retelling the story. Here are some of the questions I model with the text and the children's responses to them after the reread.

Before the second reading, I prompt the children: "On each page, ask yourself who this little girl is and who the person on the other page is. Look closely at the illustrations and listen to the word clues that Charlotte left behind."

- As I read the title and study the cover of the book, I model the language of inference: "I wonder who these people are. I think it's probably a mommy and her little girl. I'm inferring this because their hair looks the same and they're wearing the same hats. And the lady has her arm around the girl."

- After reading text on the next few pages: "I notice the little girl is pointing at a picture frame, and on this page she's looking at a book. I wonder why?"

- As I read on: "I'm thinking the little girl is looking at a book of photographs, a photo album. I'm inferring this because I see pictures in the book, and there's no writing." As I flip back to previous pages, I say: "Wait a minute . . . the photos in the picture frame look like they could be the pictures of this growing girl." I point to the opposite page and continue, "The illustrations in the picture frame are kind of fuzzy, but you can see, for example, her graduation hat and long flowing hair."

- I turn the page and read: "'This young lady laughing with those boys is my mother.' It sounds like she's describing what she sees in the photograph. I'm inferring this picture [pointing to the growing girl] is the photograph she's looking at. See the long flowing hair in the picture frame?"

On the third read-through, I use questions to teach critical reasoning and prompt children to infer for themselves. Several pages into the book, I ask, "What words do you keep hearing over and over again?"

"This . . . is my mother."

"Who is 'my mother'?"

Children point to the picture on the opposite page, of a little girl growing in size. "Yes!" I gesture toward the child on the left-hand page, who's pointing at a picture frame. "Who is this little girl?"

"It's her daughter!" they exclaim.

"Hmmm, but how can her mother be a little girl if *she's* a little girl?"

No response.

"What is the little girl pointing at?"

"A picture."

"A picture of whom?"

"Her mother!"

"What picture is the little girl looking at?"

Animatedly, they respond by pointing to the illustration on the right side of the page and connecting it to the picture frame the little girl is looking at: "That picture's in here!"

Later: "Why is this quiet lady 'lovely and large'?"

"She's pregnant!"

"With whom?"

"Her daughter!"

I read the ending of the book: "And here is where I begin. The beginning."

"In that sentence," I ask the children, "whom does *I* refer to?"

The children animatedly point to the pictures. "That's her when she was born!"

"*Her* means who?"

"The little girl!"

"Who is telling the story?" A look of confusion crosses their faces. I once again reread the first page, "This baby smiling in her bassinette under the crocheted throw," and emphasize the words "*is my mother.*"

"The little girl is telling the story!"

"Who is 'this baby smiling in her bassinette under the crocheted throw'?"

"That's her mommy when she was a baby!"

"Yes! And how was she telling the story of her mother's life?"

"Through the pictures!"

When it's time for writing, I build a bridge from our reading to the task at hand. "Today in your writing, before you pick up your pencil, think about *showing*, not *telling*, what's going on in your story. Try to leave word clues and picture clues so that your readers and listeners will have to think. Make your story interesting. Charlotte Zolotow didn't *tell* you that this was a little girl talking about her mother growing up. She left word clues, and Anita Lobel, the illustrator, left picture clues to make you think."

As children begin to work, I sit down next to Selena and ask, "So what are you writing about today, sweetheart?"

"We're moving."

"Wow . . . saying good-bye to your house and your friends can be hard." I pause and ask, "How can you show you're moving without *saying* you are? Close your eyes and tell me what you are doing."

"Me and my mom are packing my clothes."

"That's great, Selena; put that down quickly. And *where* are you packing them?"

"In boxes."

I carefully echo her words and ask, "What are you doing with the boxes?"

"Putting them in front of our house."

"That's such a great description of what's happening! You didn't come right out and *tell* the reader that you're moving. Instead, you said, 'Me and my mom are packing my clothes in boxes and putting them in front of our house.' So I can *infer* that you're moving." (See Figure 7–11.)

At another table, Anayansi is writing about what she's noticed in observing Houdinni, our garter snake, for several days. She's noticed a shift in his behavior and coloration. Based on these clues, she infers that he's beginning the molting process and records this great visual in her daybook without stating the obvious. "Houdinni is STaiNG STL. HiS BoDy iS KroLD uP iN a circle! His isz are BaBy blue!" (*Houdinni is staying still. His body is curled up in a circle! His eyes are baby blue!*) (see Figure 7–12).

RIDDLES

In the beginning weeks of our focus on inference, I model riddles several times by writing them on our morning message board (see Figure 6–8). Riddles are a fun, sim-

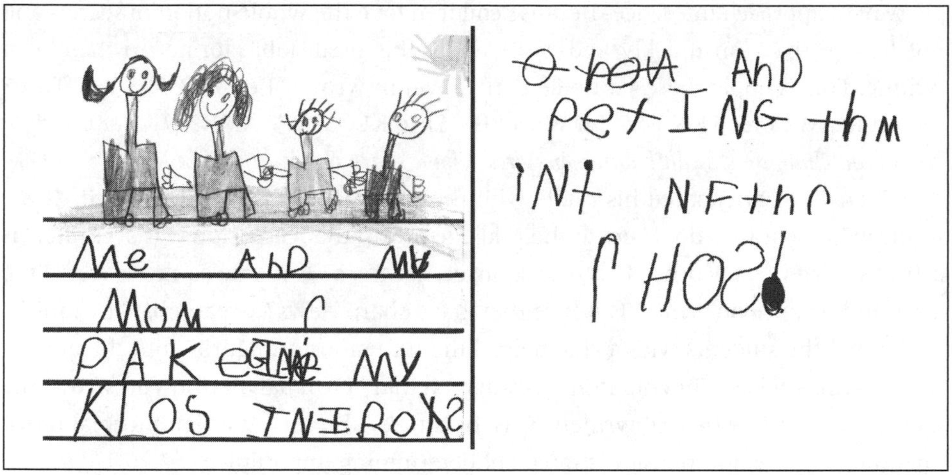

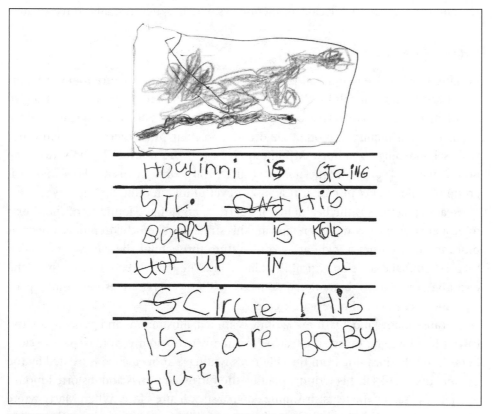

FIGURE 7–11 *Selena practices showing rather than telling:* Me and my mom are packing my clothes in boxes and putting them in front of our house!

FIGURE 7–12 *Anayansi's written observation of Houdinni the garter snake*

ple way to approach inference. Because children love the whole notion of secrets and not telling, they can quickly and easily apply this predictable format to their own writing. For example, here's a riddle that Giovanni wrote: "I eT AKORJS I eT ThreS I K An KLiM Chres I KN BLS On WIrS I HV Shrb KLOS! WT AM I? (*I eat acorns. I eat trees. I can climb trees. I can balance on wires. I have sharp claws. What am I?*).

When Giovanni shared his riddle with the group, the children responded, "It's a squirrel!" As I always do, I reread the riddle to affirm that each clue was accurate: "Is it true squirrels eat acorns? Is it true squirrels eat trees? Is it true squirrels can climb trees and balance on wires? Is it true they have sharp claws? Great job, Giovanni!"

I asked the students which clue helped them the most in figuring out the answer to Giovanni's riddle. They unanimously agreed that "I can balance on wires" was the most revealing clue he had written. This, of course, also served as an informal introduction to the comprehension strategy of determining importance.

If children guess an incorrect answer to a riddle, I encourage them to determine for themselves whether their answer is true. I might say, for example, "If *cat* is the answer to Giovanni's riddle, is it true that cats eat acorns? Is it true that cats eat trees? Is it true that they balance on wires?" This series of questions, encouraging critical reasoning, helps children decide for themselves whether their response is reasonable.

WHAT WE CAN LEARN

Because I emphasize inquiry all year long, inferring is second nature to my students and therefore not difficult for them to practice as a comprehension strategy. They've heard me model the language, so they know what it sounds like when a reader infers. Later, through inquiry, I prompt children to do their own inferring to figure out what's happening in a story. My questions about *This Quiet Lady* show how the process works. The specific questions, of course, will be unique to each book and each group of children, because their responses never unfold in quite the same way.

Reading pictures is the beginning of inferring, and I have found nonfiction texts to be a great literacy context for applying this strategy. When children have opportunities to choose from a wide array of literature throughout the day, they broaden their schema and develop critical thinking skills. They're working constantly in the cognitive, creative, and emotional domains as they generate questions and experience the excitement of new learning.

Because many kindergartners' writing is limited, illustrations and punctuation can carry a lot of weight. In fact, the teacher constantly needs to use word or picture clues herself, to infer meaning from the children's writing. I know a child is excited by the exclamation marks in his writing; mad by the furrowed brows and distorted mouth in a picture; sad by the tears streaming down a stick figure's face. When Marty wrote "RRRRRR!" in the talking bubble coming out of Killer's mouth, he not only created a mental image but helped his fellow students infer the dispositions of his two dogs, Angel and Killer. (Their names alone paint an inferential picture.)

You can encourage children to include in their drawings details like short straight lines, consecutive spirals, or curved humps, so the reader can infer movements of running or rolling or bouncing. Gina's loose tooth is a great example. Not only did she leave word clues such as *wiggly* and *moves forward and back*, but she included rich detail in her illustration: the mouth was open wide with a small amount of blood, and a series of movement lines surrounded the tooth.

Children naturally and intuitively infer every day. From a young age, they learn how to emotionally read parents, family, and friends. When Grandma smiles with both hands hidden behind her back, they infer that a surprise awaits. When familiar yummy smells come from the kitchen, they infer that a favorite meal is being prepared. When Mom has a frown, they infer that they've done something wrong. So emotions are a natural place to begin teaching inference.

Encouraging children to describe an emotion without stating it outright shifts the delivery of a story, bringing it to life. Isabella's rich description of playing and having fun with her brother, Giovanni, is a great example of this: "we roLd in are Bae Like a Brdo! we KdRT To GeT ouT! we wr aT or OLd Haosh!" (*We rolled in our blanky like a burrito! We tried to get out! We were at our old house!*) (see Figure 7–13). Lorraine, on the other hand, began by simply stating what was happening in her life: her father was getting out of jail (see Figure 7–14). I asked how she felt, encouraging her to express her emotion through words without explicitly stating joy. That's when she wrote, "I aM Fieing that IM' going to criy!" (*I am feeling that I'm going to cry!*).

My overall expectation in teaching inference is for children to orally implement the strategy across content areas and contexts, such as play. I want them to notice a friend sitting on the cement, with swelling tears and sniffles, infer that the friend is hurt, and offer support. With writing, my goal is for children to experiment with showing, rather than telling. I want all my students to be able to apply inference when reading fiction and nonfiction texts through pictures, and eventually, with support, to apply it through read-alouds and their independent reading.

Where to Start

- Reflect on how you use thinking strategies in your own reading and how they enhance comprehension for you.
- Look for ways to apply thinking strategies in all contexts of learning (sharing, community, literacy, play, science, math, social studies, art, music).
- Spend time with books you think your children will enjoy. Ask yourself:
  - What thinking strategy best demonstrates the author's craft?

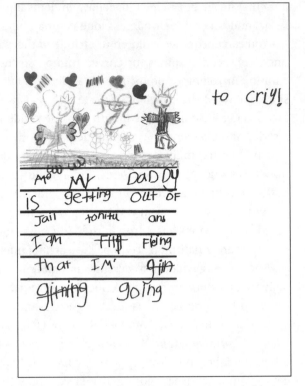

FIGURE 7–13 *Isabella's writing about having fun with her brother*

FIGURE 7–14 *Lorraine's emotional story:* My daddy is getting out of jail tonight and I am feeling that I'm going to cry!

- Does the writing provoke a powerful experience?
- Does it elicit vivid images?
- Does it cause you to ask questions?
- Do you find yourself reading between the lines?
- Organize your read-alouds according to these strategies for easy retrieval.
- Continue to search for great texts, adding to your collection.
- Network with colleagues and share titles you have found to be effective. Remember some texts will resonate for them and not for you and vice versa.

Books for Teaching Comprehension Strategies

Many engaging books we read to children can work well for modeling thinking strategies. Examine the texts you read to your students and think about how best to use them in studying a particular comprehension strategy. Often a good book will cross boundaries; for example, *The Snowy Day* (Keats 1962) works well for modeling both activating schema and creating mental images. The following lists, sorted by category and shown in most cases with increasing complexity, will give you a place to start.

Activating Schema

Bailey the Big Bully, by Lizi Boyd

When Sophie Gets Angry—Really, Really Angry, by Molly Bang

My Secret Place, by Erica Magnus

There's a Nightmare in My Closet, by Mercer Mayer

The Snowy Day, by Ezra Jack Keats

Peter's Chair, by Ezra Jack Keats

Jamaica Tag Along, by Juanita Havill

Our Granny, by Margaret Wild

Nana Upstairs and Nana Downstairs, by Tomie dePaola

Koala Lou, by Mem Fox

Creating Mental Images

A Children's Zoo, by Tana Hoban

Salt Hands, by Jane Chelsea Aragon

Green Eyes, by A. Birnbaum

The Paperboy, by Dav Pilkey

Grandfather's Trolley, by Bruce McMillan

Night in the Country, by Cynthia Rylant

Shortcut, by Donald Crews

The Snowy Day, by Ezra Jack Keats

Goggles! by Ezra Jack Keats

Fireflies! by Julie Brinckloe

Questioning

Why Is the Sky Blue? by Sally Grindley

Little Blue and Little Yellow, by Leo Lionni

Grandfather Twilight, by Barbara Berger

Lon Po Po, by Ed Young

The Other Side, by Jacqueline Woodson

Wild Horse Winter, by Tetsuya Honda

Mr. Archimedes' Bath, by Pamela Allen

The Bear and Mr. Bear, by Frances Thomas

Dear Willie Rudd, by Libba Moore Gray

Inferring

Good Dog, Carl, by Alexandra Day

Swimmy, by Leo Lionni

This Quiet Lady, by Charlotte Zolotow

A Mother for Choco, by Keiko Kasza (inference with feelings)

Something Beautiful, by Sharon Dennis Wyeth

Charlie Anderson, by Barbara Abercrombie

The Empty Pot, by Demi

See the Ocean, by Estelle Condra

Reading

After three days without reading, talk becomes flavorless.

—Chinese proverb

8

It's a sweltering day in late August. Inside our cool classroom, my lively new kindergartners are reading a passage on the message board from a classic book, *Dr. Seuss's ABC* (1963). To the tune of "Twinkle, Twinkle Little Star," we sing: "Big *A* / Little *a* / What begins with *Aa*?"

Next, my finger tracks the words in the book as we sing the rest of Dr. Seuss' *a* page together: "Big *A* / Little *a* / What begins with *Aa*? / Aunt Annie's alligator / *A*, *A*, *A*."

For those three final *a*'s, I sing the first two with the short *a* sound and the last one with the long sound, so that the children hear both sounds the vowel can make, always emphasizing sounds as opposed to letter names. (For consonants, I repeat the sound twice and then state the letter name.) Singing and writing on the message board, using each letter from the Dr. Seuss book, is one of the ways I gradually introduce my students to the alphabet. After singing, the children join me by drawing the capital and lowercase *a*'s in the air. Then I write the letters on the dry-erase board, emphasizing top-down strokes.

Next I pick up the book *The Handmade Alphabet*, by Laura Rankin (1991), and show the children how to sign the letter *a* in American Sign Language. We all practice shaping the letter with our fingers as we sing the first page of this book, "*A* for asparagus," to a simple tune I made up. In my early years of teaching, I noticed the calming effect that American Sign Language had on children, how it riveted their attention on my moving fingers and then their own. Using sign language is a natural avenue for reinforcing the identification of letters; it's another fun, kinesthetic way to learn.

The following day, the message board says:

Big B,
Little b,
What begins with Bb?

I sing and read the words on the board, introduce formation of the capital and lowercase *b*, and reread the book from the beginning. (Later in the month, as we near the midway point in *Dr. Seuss's ABC*, I switch from reviewing the whole book to reviewing only the current letter and the five most recent letters, in order to save time. Then, when we reach the letter *Z*, we read the entire book together, from start to finish.) *Dr. Seuss's ABC* becomes a seminal choice during independent reading and reading workshop for the rest of the year. Children love the book, confidently picking it up to reread time and again. As reading skills increase, many of the children expand their repertoire of sight words by singing this Dr. Seuss classic. (The primary focus in *Dr. Seuss's ABC* is to expand children's independent reading selections; it's not intended to be used as a system for introducing sounds and letters.)

■ The Big Picture

Teachers who visit my classroom share many insights, but it's their questions that always draw me in. When visitors come late in the school year, they'll say, "Gosh, your kids are such great readers; I can't believe how focused and independent they are." Then come the questions: "How do you get them to choose books on their own and find partners to read with? Do you tell them whom to read with or what books they *have* to read? Your kids are really reading *words*. How did they learn their letters and sounds? *When* did you teach them this? You have so many books in your room. How do the kids know where they all go?"

By spring my students are independently choosing a variety of texts—leveled books, songbooks, pattern and rhyme, various types of nonfiction, favorite read-aloud picture books—in ways that look amazingly smooth. If a child tries to read a book that turns out to be beyond her abilities, I encourage her to seek out a friend for help. Visitors respond to this scene with wonder, but of course the class didn't always run this way. What observers are seeing is the result of a slow process that began late the previous summer, when the group first entered my classroom. Let me give you an overall picture of what reading looks like in my room and then take you step-by-step through our morning schedule and through our year, so you can see how the pieces fit together and knit over time into a coherent whole.

I design the kindergarten day with two separate reading periods, settling-in time and reading workshop, with a specific purpose for each. During settling-in time, first thing in the morning, my students are free to choose what they want to read, alone or with partners. This independent reading focuses primarily on making sense of whole texts, not on decoding individual words. Later, in reading workshop, we flip the focus, concentrating more on making sense at the word level. To become good readers, of course, students need both sets of skills.

Independent reading sets the stage for learning in all three domains: cognitive, creative, and emotional. During this time, children are questioning, reasoning, inferring, and using their background knowledge to make sense of a text as a whole. They're exploring new discoveries with others, expanding vocabulary and schema with friends, and sharing their excitement about reading and learning.

Independent reading time keeps Ms. Lisa and me busy listening to the children, helping with vocabulary, and encouraging readers to teach others what they are thinking and learning: a piece of new information they've gained from a nonfiction book, a question they're wondering about, or a new song or pattern book they've mastered. To a casual observer, settling-in time may not look significant, but in fact it's a consistent part of our daily schedule and an important part of students' overall reading time.

Years ago—before DRA started, before expectations for kindergarten began rising higher and higher each year—my primary focus in teaching reading was having students derive meaning from whole text. I did much of that work during writing time as a modeled read-aloud, as described in the previous chapter. I still follow that practice, but now I'm also careful to spend considerable time helping students make meaning on a word level. Like it or not, that's what the district mandates. We all need to find a balance between meeting our own goals and living within the system by ensuring that tests give our students credit for what they know. The focus of this chapter is to show how to apply the comprehension strategies and the three domains on a word level in teaching reading. Because I teach so many reading skills in a writing context, reading workshop becomes the time for the children to practice those skills independently. I'll begin chronologically, showing you how our reading workshop gains complexity as the year progresses.

In the first six weeks of our reading workshop, I'm busy teaching children reading behaviors and familiarizing them with how books are arranged in the classroom. I gradually introduce children to different kinds of books, and I model how to read nonfiction texts. I also introduce a letter and sound system, which integrates visual, kinesthetic, and auditory components. Each letter has a picture depicting the letter's sound and an associated movement; these are the sound cards to which children refer all year long. Letter sounds are introduced in a certain order, beginning with continuous sounds—such as /s/, /m/, and /f/—as opposed to stop sounds—such as /b/, /k/, and /p/—which are more difficult to pronounce (Sousa 2005).

So, for example, when I reread a page in *Dr. Seuss's ABC*, "Big *H*, little *h*, Hungry horse. Hay. Hen in a hat. Hooray! Hooray!" I pick up the sound card and point to *H*, "Hh." We all pump our arms like the out-of-breath runner in the picture as we pant, "Huh, huh, *h*." By the time we near the end of the ABC book, the children know the movements and sounds associated with the letters; their minds link each sound card to that letter's page in the book.

Early in the year, because introducing the letter-sound system and familiarizing children with reading behaviors takes so long, children's actual reading time lasts just ten to fifteen minutes. The time gradually increases, until by March children read for thirty to thirty-five minutes.

My goal at the beginning of the year is to quickly build a repertoire of books the children are familiar with and can read independently. I focus first on wordless, ABC, song, and counting books, and introduce others—pattern, rhyme, leveled text—as the children gradually gain competence and confidence.

Those modest goals are a starting point for the children as we begin the year. Kindergarten is the first formal school setting for half the children in my class, and many have had only limited experience with books. My list of reading goals for the full year is far more extensive and aims to tap all three domains:

- explore a variety of texts (creative domain)
- reread favorite read-alouds through pictures (cognitive domain)
- understand procedures and behavioral characteristics of successful readers (cognitive domain)
- enjoy the process of reading (emotional domain)
- stimulate questions and make new discoveries (cognitive and creative domains)
- expand schema and nurture a desire to learn (cognitive, creative, and emotional domains)
- create sensory images while reading (cognitive domain)
- infer while reading (cognitive domain)
- comprehend meaning behind the whole text (cognitive and creative domains)
- build fluency (creative domain)
- apply what has been learned in writing to reading (cognitive domain)

■ Rhythm in Reading

One early October day, I keep the steady beat with an egg shaker as I read my class Sue Williams' big book *I Went Walking* (1989). "I went walking; what did I see? I saw a black cat looking at me. I went walking; what did I see? I saw a brown horse looking at me."

Tiny beads inside the egg shaker rattle softly—*chh, chh, chh*—defining the underlying pulse of the sentences: *I* went *walk*-ing; *what* did I *see*? (The italics indicate my downbeats.)

After reading each page, I have the children echo my words, keeping the steady beat for themselves by gently slapping their thighs with both hands. Then I reread the book from start to finish as the children echo and clap with *each* syllable of text; that's how they demonstrate rhythm.

Though it may not look that way, we're having a lesson on reading fluency. Developing steady beat and rhythm—by singing, clapping, and echoing—stimulates the process of linking language to print. This foundation in music strengthens fluency and comprehension when reading texts, so that children can focus more on meaning and less on decoding. When children are exposed to music at an early age, they enter school having already internalized the concepts of steady beat (the underlying pulse) and rhythm (syllabic representation). "Studies have found that the sense of steady pulse and rhythm increases phonological awareness, including rhyme and alliteration. In addition, research has confirmed the use of songs in aiding the realization of phonemic awareness" (Womack 2006, 19).

When children are chanting and clapping a book, the text comes alive. Along with the rhythm, they internalize the idea of intonation, increasing the chance that they'll learn to read with feeling rather than in a robotic monotone. For these reasons, I make rhythmic experiences a primary focus in reading workshop at the start of the year and also incorporate them throughout the day, for example, with math chants at the beginning of math time, lullabies to sooth a dolly during dramatic play, or songs and rhymes after recess.

I begin the year reinforcing steady beat when we sing or march. Children hear me say, "Keep the steady beat," as I clap my hands or tap my thighs. I encourage everyone to mimic my movements, and then I increase the complexity, adding rhythm sticks and egg shakers. Rhymes are a great place to begin contrasting steady beat with rhythm while teaching traditional text structures. Many children, however, have not encountered the standard repertoire; something as simple as "One, Two, Buckle My Shoe" may be completely foreign to them. It's especially important to help these children link steady beat and rhythm so they can transfer those elements to reading. Not knowing traditional rhymes can cause problems because these are the rhymes most often put into print for children to read.

Initially, children echo small chunks of the rhyme as I gesture with both pointer fingers. I encourage them to maintain a steady beat with both hands on their thighs as we recite together. Next I contrast steady beat with rhythm, which the children and I demonstrate by echoing small chunks of rhyme and clapping the beat on every syllable. Each time we recite a rhyme, we define and differentiate steady beat and rhythm through both language and movement. By the end of the year, students have a firm grasp of using steady beat and rhythm through shared reading. One day in early spring I saw Haley, Anayansi, and Adol reading *Way Down South* (Williams 1994e). Their hands were slapping their thighs and the text simultaneously, keeping the steady beat, as they collectively sang, "*Way* down *south* where ba-*na*-nas *grow*, a *grass*-hopper *stepped* on an *ele*-phant's *toe* . . ."

■ From Pictures to Text

Like understanding rhythm, making sense of pictures is an essential behind-the-scenes skill for emerging readers. Just as children who haven't had much exposure to music will need more help with rhythm, children who haven't had much exposure to books will need more support getting started. Making sense of pictures, the first step in reading, doesn't come naturally to everyone. We must teach this skill if we want to help children experience the wonder and empowerment created when they engage independently with books. Even when they're reading only the pictures, they begin to understand relationships and make sense of the world by operating from the three domains. They wonder, discover, and feel through paying attention to details in photographs and illustrations.

"Boys and girls," I say one day in early September, "see these soft-covered books on this tall rack over here? They're called magazines, and they're about different kinds of animals. You're not going to be reading the magazines the same way you would *Mary Wore Her Red Dress*. Instead, when you read them, pay close attention to the detail in the illustrations and photographs. Keep asking yourself questions and thinking about what you know."

This is how I introduce nonfiction texts and help children see that reading them will be a little different from what they've done before. *Mary Wore Her Red Dress* (Peek 1998) is a pattern song book, a predictable, fun introduction to colors and animals. It's one of the first books we read in class because it's easy; all the children have to do is look at the picture clues, remember the pattern, and sing. Reading nonfiction, in contrast, requires more intense observation and many more strategies: using your background knowledge, asking questions, inferring. So I want to the children to start flipping down new lenses for this new way of looking at texts.

I pick up a *Zoobooks* magazine about crocodiles and talk about what I see. By thinking aloud, I'm modeling how to ask questions and make sense of the illustrations. "This alligator can see a lion from far away because his eyes are on top of his head. And from this picture, it looks like the alligator takes a deep breath and swims under water, sneaking up on the lion, and pops up out of the water and attacks him! I wonder who usually wins those fights?"

Sharing our thinking builds community, which in turn expands learning and possibilities. So I tell the students, "When you discover something, I want you to turn to someone nearby and share your thinking. Tap that person gently on the shoulder and say, 'Look what I discovered! Alligators can sneak up on lions under the water and attack them.' What's really fun is you're going to be teaching and learning so much from one another. Ms. Lisa and I want to hear you thinking out loud."

Though I incorporate the language of inference when speaking with children all year long, I wait until springtime to introduce inference as a formal comprehension strategy. For example, if I revisited this particular *Zoobooks* magazine in the spring, I might say, "I'm inferring the lion can't see the eyes of the alligator from a distance, and that's why the alligator can get close and surprise the lion. A lion would never let another animal attack him knowingly!"

When I first model how to read nonfiction, however, my instructions are much more basic. "In many magazines, you're going to see really cool things you don't understand," I tell the group. "Remember to stop and ask questions. Do you ever keep reading when you don't understand?"

"No!" the children answer with authority.

"If you don't understand, then turn to a buddy and say, 'I don't understand this picture; do *you* get it?' If your buddy can't help you, don't stop there. Ask another friend, or ask me or Ms. Lisa. During reading today, along with songbooks, ABC books, and wordless books, you might want to choose a *Zoobooks* magazine."

■ Reading Workshop

As children filter through the doorway after our morning recess, they hear a much-loved song coming from the CD player. Settling back into the classroom, we all sing "Everything Grows" as my finger tracks the words in a book. Music and songs help smooth transitions while effortlessly and gently calming children (see Figure 8–1).

Rhymes, rhythms, and finger plays also engage young children. Not only are they fun and comforting, but they encourage focus and strengthen internal language patterns, auditory skills, and eye-hand coordination. Songs and rhymes preface our reading workshop. Here's a favorite rhyme we recite together, after learning it in small chunks:

> Let your hands go clap, clap, clap. Let your fingers go snap, snap, snap. Let
> your lips go very round [form the lips in a circle], but do not make a sound
> [hold pointer finger perpendicular to the lips]. Fold your hands. Close each
> eye. Take a deep breath, and softly sigh [let out a gentle *ahh*].

By the end of these tranquilizing rhymes, most of the children have their listening eyes turned toward me; they're ready to move on. Our reading workshop has

FIGURE 8–1 *Children settle in for reading workshop with a song.*

the same three elements as our writing workshop: a minilesson, guided independent practice, and a share. We begin with shared reading, which can take the form of a big book or chanting rhymes and singing songs from chart paper. Early in the year, reading workshop focuses on building oral language, developing fluency, and modeling concepts of print like left-to-right progression, return sweep, and voice-print match.

I keep a fun, interactive feel to our reading workshop. Songbooks, wordless books, pattern books, counting books, jump rope rhymes, leveled texts, an assortment of nonfiction texts, and *Zoobooks* magazines are arranged in colorful tubs on the floor, clearly labeled for easy access. After shared reading, children are free to choose from all these tubs and choose partners to read with, as long as they are thoughtful about their choices. Body language and tone of voice are just two of the hints that tell me whether or not reading is going well.

Because we accomplish so much of our literacy work during writing workshop (through read-aloud or modeled writing, guided independent practice, and author's share) and during interactive writing on the dry-erase board, our reading workshop becomes the time for independent practice of those skills. Children revisit the skills by integrating them in a reading context, thus building confidence. For example, if they've been working on using periods ("stops") in their writing, then in reading they practice making their voices stop when they see that dot at the end of a sentence. I encourage children to talk, sing, and interact with texts in a free-flowing manner and to share questions and discoveries with others. Table 8–1 is a general guideline for introducing skills. It is not intended to apply to all children; order and timing will vary with the population.

Minilessons

The reading minilesson is brief and takes many different forms. Sometimes we begin with a big book or a song or rhyme that we chant together from the large chart stand. Other times, I have one child or several come to the front of the class to be guest readers who will teach their classmates about the conventions of print. They introduce a new book they have learned to read and model for others what a good reader does. This sets classroom expectations and acknowledges children in front of their peers, building confidence and reinforcing necessary skills in a child-centered manner.

For example, one day after Alicia came to the front and read a book about baby animals, I asked the rest of the children, "So what did you notice Alicia doing?" The question was deliberately open-ended to encourage children to focus on any reading behaviors that struck them. Here are some of the students' responses:

She read the title.
She pointed to the words as she was reading.
She turned the pages slowly.
She looked like she was thinking.
Her eyes were on the pictures and the words.
She reread when she got confused.
She looked at the picture and the letter to figure out the word.

I make a chart listing specific reading behaviors I want to encourage and add to it as the year progresses. Whenever possible, I praise a child in the moment for demonstrating a desired reading behavior, then write this attribute on the chart. Here is a sample of a classroom chart titled "What Good Readers Do":

- Pick a book they know how to read or want to read
- Find the title and read it
- Open the book and turn the pages slowly and carefully
- Put their eyes on the pictures and words
- Slide their pointer finger under words and talk

Skill	Beginning	Middle	End
TABLE 8–1 *Quick Reference Chart for Skill Introduction*			
Reading behaviors: • handling books • turning pages with pointer finger and thumb • locating front and back of book • locating title of book • determining where eyes belong while reading • thinking aloud • sitting with a book • finding a reading spot	x		
Organization of texts	x		
Selection and proper return of texts	x		
Becoming familiar with text structures: • wordless books • ABC books • songbooks • counting books • leveled texts • pattern books • rhymed texts	x		
Introducing the letter-sound system	x		
How to read wordless books	x		
How to read nonfiction text	x	x	
How to reread a favorite picture book through illustrations	x	x	
Concepts of print: • left-to-right progression • voice-print match • return sweep • punctuation (form and function) • "first" and "last" on a sentence and word level (i.e., first letter in word, or first word in sentence, and so on) • distinguishing between a letter and a word	x	x	

Skill	Beginning	Middle	End
TABLE 8–1 *Quick Reference Chart for Skill Introduction*			
Locating sight words in context by framing them with pointer fingers	x	x	x
Determining how many words one hears, or reads, in a sentence		x	x
Using picture and letter clues to decode unknown words	x	x	x
Incorporating thinking strategies on a word level: • activating schema • creating mental images • questioning • inferring		x	x
Incorporating thinking strategies on a whole-text level: • activating schema • creating mental images • questioning • inferring (See Chapter 7 for more details.)	x	x	x
Strengthening visual memory of words: • magnetic letters • writing words with pointer finger on table and palm of other hand • covering illustration with construction paper and working with text alone (advanced readers)		x	x
Summarizing and retelling a story (becomes more sophisticated as year progresses)	x	x	x
Selecting text		x	x
Working with word families to increase awareness of rhyming, sight words, and spelling		x	x

- Think!
- Reread
- Use their schema: think about what they already know and what the reading reminds them of
- Visualize: make pictures in their head
- Ask questions
- Infer: use pictures and letters to figure out words

The minilessons emphasize different skills at different times. Early in the year I focus on reading behavior—what students should hear and see during reading workshop. I model specific book-handling skills:

- how to find the front of the book
- how to locate and identify the title
- how to turn pages with pointer finger and thumb
- where their eyes belong
- what their mind should be doing while they are looking at pictures
- how to put books away with the title facing out

Later, minilessons take up more sophisticated skills: left-to-right progression, return sweep, voice-print match, reading a story through pictures, and reinforcing high-frequency sight words.

Guided Practice: First Half of Year

After I've set the context for reading and modeled what good reading looks and sounds like, children begin to demonstrate their independence as readers. From the way they choose and handle books, find a reading spot, focus their eyes on the text, and return books to their proper tubs, I can tell when they're ready for more. Next we tackle content, such as reading nonfiction texts and talking about them, and we build a repertoire of pattern books that the children can successfully read.

Because children love singing, songbooks are a great place to start. These texts typically have embedded patterns that make it easy for children to master skills like sight-word identification, steady beat, and rhythm. Four tubs of songbooks are clumped together on the floor of my classroom for easy retrieval and return (see Figure 8–2). Each tub contains multiple copies of some books, promoting small-group sharing. After I teach children a song, they immediately gravitate toward songbooks during reading time, singing and reading fluently alongside peers.

Starting the year with fun, lively songbooks, rather than leveled books with three to four words on a page, builds confidence and fluency among my young readers. In addition, longer songbooks extend embedded language structures, exposing children

FIGURE 8–2 *Songbook tubs*

FIGURE 8–3 *Tubs for leveled texts and various other book categories*

to the more sophisticated sentence constructions they will encounter in future reading. As the year progresses, I set out and integrate additional tubs of predictable, pattern, and leveled texts as part of the repertoire of choice texts.

Usually I introduce leveled books about three months into school, when children are beginning to identify simple sight words. I introduce "blue dot" books first, handing a different book to each child as we sit on the oval. I shake my tambourine, signaling the start of a quick read. Children quickly peruse a book and then pass it to their left when my tambourine sounds again. This is a fast, fun way for children to familiarize themselves with a broad selection of books.

A good organization system is essential for helping children retrieve and return books efficiently. Right now my system is organized by colored dots: Blue dots are the simplest books (three to four words on a page with no return sweep, and a one-word change on each page), followed by yellow dots and red dots. Green-dot books are the most difficult (see Figure 8–3). Whenever I talk about the categories, I refer to the number of words on a page, not to "hard" or "easy" reading. I introduce leveled books for reading selection gradually and then rotate them to another part of the classroom or the back closet when they become too simple.

When watching the children's interaction with books, I reinforce positive behaviors to strengthen self-esteem and independence. This is especially important because of the limited exposure many of my students have had to books before arriving in my classroom. Modeling expectations, reinforcing reading behaviors, and building reading stamina are yearlong goals.

To help build stamina, I acknowledge specific behaviors, often commenting on them as I read with a small group. "Great job, Giovanni and Abdili. You guys are doing awesome reading together. I love how you both have your fingers on the words. When you're finished, ask Tyberius and Gonzalo if they'd like to learn to read your book." They respond with smiles and nods.

"Great reading, Shannon! You keep going, hon!"

"Selena, you're doing a wonderful job reading that dinosaur book. Remember, I want you reading books in which you can read the *words* too, now."

In front of our big-block area, I notice three girls sitting together on a long wooden bench, holding multiple copies of the same book. "Wow, girls, I can't believe you can read *The Lady with the Alligator Purse* all by yourselves. You are so smart!"

Nearby, Passion is distracted and staring off into space with a pile of books beside her. "Sweetheart, go over and join the girls. Remember, that's the book you wanted to learn to read yesterday." Passion takes my advice and soon becomes engaged with the other three. (See Figure 8–4.)

Every day I confer with children individually, monitor small groups that have

FIGURE 8–4 *Julia, Isabella, and Lorraine read independently.*

FIGURE 8–5 *A small group reads with multiple copies.*

formed independently, or pull aside children needing work with specific skills such as voice-print match, locating sight words in context, or deciphering words using word or picture clues. In addition, I may form a focused group to assess those skills or to introduce a new song or predictable book. (See Figure 8–5.)

The key to all of this is letting children choose their own reading material. Children who self-select texts are much more focused and invested in reading. Trusting a child to choose books or reading partners builds confidence, accessing the emotional domain. On any given day, of course, some children will choose books that are too hard or too easy. I take time to guide them through the process, helping them find books that match their reading level and interest. I suggest they put a selection of books in their cubby for easy retrieval during reading time, and I support them in rotating the collection when they lose interest in certain titles. I also encourage each child to include more challenging texts. (See Figure 8–6.)

Everything we do in reading workshop aims to create a tone of independence, excitement, purpose, and reciprocity. "We are all teachers and learners," I regularly tell the group. Children's self-esteem increases when they share knowledge with others, and community strengthens when they rely on friends as resources. You know your children are invested in reading when they call out their enthusiasm for discoveries they've made from fiction or nonfiction; when they reread favorite books with confidence and gusto; or when they sing with peers while poring over the printed

FIGURE 8–6 *Adol and Julia read self-selected texts together.*

text of a treasured song. My goal is to instill a sense of wonder and a love for books, to introduce each child to the gifts hidden between the pages.

Guided Practice: Second Half of Year

As the weather warms to spring, the climate in our classroom changes as well. Rather than sticking with the books they already know how to read, students are selecting texts outside their comfort zone (though the familiar nonfiction texts and songbooks are still available for choice). On a word level, we begin incorporating an array of strategies—activating schema, questioning, creating mental images, and inferring—for decoding language and comprehending text. For example, a child uses several strategies when he stops and questions an unknown word, skips it and reads on, then goes back to reread and manages to infer the word's meaning from context and letter and picture clues.

For many, spring is the time when reading really begins to click in and DRA levels advance. As children learn more sight words and more strategies for deciphering words they don't know, they build confidence, which in turn increases their willingness to choose more challenging texts. They realize that they have begun to understand words and meaning; they're not just relying on patterned structures to recite.

When children encounter difficult words as they read, I introduce more sophisticated strategies, such as recognizing and understanding compound words and contractions or identifying root words with endings. These skills are appropriate for my advanced readers but are not intended for all, so I address them in a small group.

On Friday, our flex day, we deviate from the traditional routine of writing workshop and spend time focusing on other experiences such as drawing, printing, and cooking. (See Chapter 2 for my weekly schedule.) Frequently, these activities are followed by an extended reading time, adding a smooth transition to the morning activities and giving children additional freedom to choose books and partners. Friday reading time is similar to our early-morning independent reading time and less structured than a reading workshop.

One spring day as I listen to Auriyah fondly reread *Martin's Big Words* (Rappaport 2001), I'm surprised when she stops and reads the word *people*. "Wow, how did you know that word?" I ask.

She quietly responds, "I knew it from 'May All Children,'" referring to a song about September 11 that we've sung from chart paper. It is through connecting words in all contexts that children increase sight vocabulary. My students love to spot familiar words on song charts, in the title of a read-aloud, or in a friend's book. "There's *like*!" or "There's *look*!" they'll shout. Or, when a friend can't recall the name of an animal in a book, "That's a *sloth*!" It's important to continually acknowledge a child's thinking in the moment, reinforcing word identification and collaboration with friends.

In the last month of school, I set aside two days during the week when the children who are ready can choose either to write or to read for an extended period (forty-five minutes to an hour). I individualize instruction and support children's personal interests, such as writing and publishing books or reading more difficult text. Those who are mature and independent enough to handle this choice experience the power of their own learning.

Small-Group Support

Under my supervision, Ms. Lisa is responsible for five or six of my least experienced learners during reading workshop. We can usually identify this group after a month or so of school, as we notice strengths and weaknesses among the children. If I didn't have my paraprofessional, I would train a parent to instruct the small group.

Most minilessons are demonstrated to the whole class. Then the small group gathers at a round table, where Ms. Lisa introduces a simple leveled text. After the children collectively read the book through a picture walk, she reads the text aloud and passes out multiple copies, encouraging children to read at their own pace as she listens. To help the group start and end smoothly, we store each child's books in a plastic bag, with the child's name on front, in a tub beneath the table. The books rotate as the year progresses.

Ms. Lisa encourages children to independently reread other familiar books in their bags and to choose longer texts, such as songbooks. This strengthens reading fluency,

FIGURE 8–7 *Ms. Lisa works with a small group while I rotate among the rest of the children.*

self-esteem, and understanding of concepts of print like return sweep, or first word and last word. For example, when singing and reading *Mary Wore Her Red Dress* (Peek 1998), the students know that their finger should begin by pointing to the first word, *Mary*, and end by pointing to the last word, *long*. Ms. Lisa and I talk daily to review which skills need emphasis and plan the next steps. Regular communication helps us support each child and keep instruction consistent. (See Figure 8–7.)

If the children in the larger group have books set aside, they store them in their hallway cubbies. They do this only if they want to or if an individual needs more structure. Generally I find children selecting texts that are right for them and forming groups of their own interests. Supporting children in selecting books is a continuing process whose value far outweighs the convenience of mandating which texts need to be in their hands. Organizing books within the small and large group helps children retrieve and return them efficiently.

Follow-Up Minilessons: First Half of Year

Minilessons in this section during this part of the year are listed here by level of difficulty. Except for the ABC booklets, all skills are introduced to all students, though the order may change based on a child's performance and needs.

When it becomes clear that some children need more support, I assign Ms. Lisa to begin small-group work by making ABC booklets with these children in order to help them with letter recognition, formation, and sounds. These booklets are prebound; each page has a capital and lowercase letter and room for a picture.

- *ABC booklets*: Children glue down a picture beginning with a letter and trace the capital and lowercase letter with their finger using top-down strokes. At the same time, they say the letter's sound twice and then the letter name ("Buh, buh, *b*."). They repeat this exercise twice. The third time, they trace the letter and say the letter sound once, then run their finger under the picture and say the name of the object shown. For example, "Buh … *bat*." Each day, they reread previous pages for reinforcement and add an additional letter to their repertoire. When children have completed the ABC booklet, and have confidently mastered identifying letters and their sounds out of sequence, they take their book home. Ms. Lisa then reviews identification of letters and sounds periodically, reinforcing retention.

- *Concepts of print* (left-to-right progression, return sweep, voice-print match, etc.): For example, I might say, "Put your fingers around the first word on this page; put your fingers around the last word on this page. Find a word that begins with the letter *r*; find a word that ends with the letter *s*." In teaching the concepts *first* and *last*, I use those words and also the words *begin* and *end*, to reinforce comprehension of terms. Focusing on concepts of print can happen during shared reading of a big book, a song or rhyme on chart paper, or an individual text.

- *Distinguishing words*: I demonstrate finding small words in a sentence by framing them with both pointer fingers (putting left and right pointer fingers around the word) in a big book text, always distinguishing between an individual letter and a *word*, a group of letters with spaces on either side. I periodically encourage children to find words in the same manner while reading in a small group, individually, or on a chart.

- *Segmenting sentences into words*: I have children count how many words they hear in a sentence; this generally falls between three and six words. When kids aurally distinguish numbers of words, this can lead later to more accurate identification of individual sounds (Sousa 2005). In my experience, when children orally identify a number of words in a sentence, they begin to generalize this skill to their writing by leaving spaces.

- *Talking about letters and sounds*: I continually talk about letters and sounds as children find words in print. For example, as children frame the word *kangaroo*, I ask, "How did you know that was *kangaroo*?"

    "Because it begins with a *k*, and I see one hopping," they reply.

    "And how else did you know it was *kangaroo*? What sound do you hear at the end of the word?"

    "*Oo*."

    "And what two letters make that sound?"

    "*O-o*, just like *boo*!"

- *Leveled texts*: I introduce leveled texts in a small group as additional choices for reading. Then I encourage children to teach others how to read them.

Follow-Up Minilessons: Second Half of Year

By the middle of the year, children are building a repertoire of books they can read and words they can identify. I use magnetic letters to strengthen visual memory of high-frequency words (Richardson 2005). (Storing the letters on a cookie sheet in ABC order is a great way to organize.) As I attach lowercase letters to a magnetic board to form a word for the large group, the children recite the letters with me, paying close attention to the number of letters and their order. Then I scramble the letters and remove one; the children figure out which one is missing from the word. I repeat the exercise, removing different letters from the word, and then have the children tell me how to reconstruct the word. This exercise is even more effective with a small group because children have more opportunities for interaction. After a child reconstructs the word, I remove the letters and all children write the word on whiteboards from memory. In addition, I ask children to use a finger to write the word on the table and on the palm of their other hand.

Another strategy for reinforcing visual memory and decoding words is to have children cover an illustration with a piece of construction paper as they read, so that they must rely solely on print. This exercise is appropriate toward the end of the year and not intended for an emergent reader who needs to focus on picture and letter clues to decipher a word.

Summarizing the main idea and retelling a story (describing the beginning, middle, and end) are skills I model all year long through read-alouds. In the second half of the year my descriptions become fuller; I want my mature readers to apply this skill to their independent reading. I ask questions like "So what's the story all about? Tell me what happened in the beginning . . . middle . . . and end." When children attempt to recapture the entire story, I stop them and ask, "What's the most important thing that happened at the beginning of the book?" This is an example of integrating the thinking strategy determining importance without conducting a formal lesson on it.

When children have trouble capturing a story sequentially, I ask about the beginning and the end, which usually makes the middle become clear. We then review what happened in sequential order and talk about the overall meaning we can take away from the story, which introduces the process of synthesis.

As children gain independence with reading, I begin guiding them to select just the right books for them. To help with this process, try the five-finger rule: As students read one page, they use their fingers to count unknown words. If they raise no fingers and make no mistakes, the book is too easy; if they count one or two unknown words on a page, the book is just right; and if all five fingers go up, the book is too challenging. Of course, just right involves not just decoding but comprehending. A book is just right if the reader can say, "I can read most words and it makes sense to me."

As reading levels advance, I integrate more work with word families, increasing awareness of rhyming, sight words, and spelling. We do this throughout the day, in our dry-erase board work, a reading minilesson, or in the middle of choice time. "If you know how to spell *at*, how would you spell *bat*, *rat*, *mat*, or *fat*? If you know to spell *day*, how would you spell *may*, *play*, or *stay*?"

Reader's Share: Learning from Others

I end the reading workshop by turning off the lights, signaling the children to freeze and look at me for direction. "Guys, please put your books away, with the titles facing out, and join us in the oval for our reader's share." I switch the lights back on as the children scurry about the room, returning texts to their proper tubs while "Love Is," one of our favorite songs, blares from the CD. By the middle of the song, children are on their bottoms, swaying and singing with arms around one another, ready for the share.

Sharing at the end of reading time is an expected part of the workshop model. Because the majority of texts the children are reading are simple, I generally use this time to model expected reading behaviors and familiarize children with text structures or identify embedded patterns and sight words by choosing a child to share a new book that he has learned to read. However, sometimes when a child is reading something more sophisticated, or rereading a picture book I have read aloud, the share lends itself to an important discovery. Kasmira's question about the snail's foot in Chapter 1 is a good example of how this happens.

After the reading share, we applaud and all say in American Sign Language: "It's time to eat lunch now. Please line up quietly." While standing in line, children snap their fingers, counting backward as we collectively recite, "Fifteen, fourteen, thirteen . . . ," increasing in speed when we reach "ten, nine, eight" and whispering on "zero." (Early in the year we count backward from ten to zero, then graduate to fifteen, then twenty, and by the end of the year we reach twenty-five.) This ritual is a calming segue to lunch and reinforces an important math skill children need to master.

■ Assessment

I evaluate children's reading accomplishments throughout the year through formal assessments like the DRA 2 and a series of ten subtests. These subtests, divided between the first and second half of the year, include word analysis assessments that measure many skills:

- identifying rhyming words through pictures
- identifying initial sounds of pictured words
- isolating the initial sound of a word
- understanding words used to talk about printed language concepts, such as *name*, *first*, *last*, *letter*, and *capital* or *uppercase letter*
- identifying capital letters within a timed period of a minute and half
- identifying lowercase letters within a timed period of a minute and half
- understanding words used to talk about printed language concepts, such as *word*, *letter*, *last*, *begin*, *end*, and *sound*
- identifying high-frequency words within a timed period of a minute and a half
- segmenting sentences into words (identifying number of words in a given sentence)
- accurately spelling two- and three-letter high-frequency words with common spelling patterns

I continually assess letter-sound identification and sight words with my least experienced learners to monitor growth and to identify areas that need more support. The child's word card list is a quick assessment tool for a general indication of reading level. For example, a child who can identify ten to twelve words is a DRA level 2, and a child who can identify sixteen to nineteen words is a DRA level 3, the expected reading level for kindergartners in our district at the end of the year.

I informally assess children by observing how they interact with text independently, what level of text they progress to (from simple predictable texts to more complicated ones), what strategies they use to make sense of what they're reading, and whether they use peers for support. These informal assessments yield the most valuable insights, indicating both strengths and areas that need work.

▧ Where to Start

- Begin encouraging children to ask questions (cognitive domain) and share new learning with others (creative domain). Continually acknowledge children for their accomplishments and support them when encountering new text (emotional domain).

- Inventory the books in your classroom. Are you offering children a broad mixture of texts from which to choose (e.g., song, ABC, wordless, pattern, rhyme, leveled, nonfiction)?

- Buy books to expand the collection in areas that are lacking. If money is an issue, order books with another teacher and rotate them between rooms.

- Organize books in a child-friendly, accessible manner.

- Find a balance between letting children select their own books and helping them find what's appropriate.

- Develop structures to help struggling readers—small-group support, repetition of needed skills, and so on.

Books for Reading Instruction

Your classroom library should include a variety of texts. Here are some suggested titles, listed by alpha order, in different genres to get you started. This list is in no way meant to be inclusive. The categories are much more important than the individual titles.

Songbooks

All the Pretty Little Horses, illustrated by Linda Saport
The Bear Went Over the Mountain, adapted by Rozanne Lanczak Williams
Bingo, illustrated by Hans Wilhelm
The Bugs Go Marching, adapted by Rozanne Lanczak Williams
Cat Goes Fiddle-I-Fee, by Paul Galdone
Down by the Bay, by Raffi
Five Little Ducks, by Raffi
Hush Little Baby Illustrated, by Shari Halpern
The Lady with the Alligator Purse, adapted and illustrated by Nadine Bernard Westcott
Mary Wore Her Red Dress, adapted and illustrated by Merle Peek
Oh, A-Hunting We Will Go, by John Langstaff
Over in the Meadow, by Paul Galdone
Peanut Butter and Jelly, illustrated by Nadine Bernard Westcott
Round and Round the Seasons Go, by Rozanne Lanczak Williams
Skip Count Song, by Rozanne Lanczak Williams
Spider on the Floor, by Raffi
Ten Monsters in a Bed, adapted by Rozanne Lanczak Williams
Today Is Monday, by Eric Carle
Way Down South, adapted by Rozanne Lanczak Williams
Wheels on the Bus, by Raffi
Who Took the Cookies from the Cookie Jar? by Rozanne Lanczak Williams

Jump Rope Rhymes

Big Fat Hen, by Keith Baker

Cinderella Dressed in Yellow, adapted by Rozanne Lanczak Williams

Miss Mary Mack, by Nadine Bernard Westcott

Teddy Bear, Teddy Bear Illustrated, by Michael Hague

ABC Books

ABC I Like Me, by Nancy Carlson

The Accidental Zucchini, by Max Grover

Alphabatics, by Suse MacDonald

Animalia, by Graeme Base

Anno's Alphabet, by Mitsumasa Anno

The Butterfly Alphabet, by Kjell B. Sandved

Chicka Chicka Boom Boom, by Bill Martin Jr. and John Archambault

Dr. Seuss's ABC, by Dr. Seuss

Eating the Alphabet, by Lois Ehlert

The Handmade Alphabet, by Laura Rankin

Have You Ever Seen . . . ? An ABC Book by Beau Gardner

On Market Street, by Arnold Lobel

Sesame Street Sign Language ABC with Linda Bove, by Linda Bove

26 Letters and 99 Cents, by Tana Hoban

V Is for Vanishing, by Patricia Mullins

The Z Was Zapped, by Chris Van Allsburg

Wordless Books

The Apple Bird, by Brian Wildsmith

A Boy, a Dog, and a Frog, by Mercer Mayer

Do You Want to Be My Friend? by Eric Carle

Early Morning in the Barn, by Nancy Tafuri

Exactly the Opposite, by Tana Hoban

Good Dog, Carl series, by Alexandra Day

Good Night, Gorilla, by Peggy Rathmann

I Read Symbols, by Tana Hoban

Look! Look! Look! by Tana Hoban

The Nest, by Brian Wildsmith

Of Colors and Things, by Tana Hoban

Pancakes for Breakfast, by Tomie dePaola

The Trunk, by Brian Wildsmith

Counting

Anno's Counting Book, by Mitsumasa Anno
Apples, by Samantha Berger and Betsey Chessen
Can You Imagine . . . ? A Counting Book, by Beau Gardner
Counting Penguins, by Betsey Chessen and Pamela Chanko
Counting Wildflowers, by Bruce McMillan
Demi's Count the Animals 1 2 3, by Demi
Fish Eyes: A Book You Can Count On, by Lois Ehlert
Moja Means One, by Muriel Feelings
Numbers All Around, by Susan Canizares and Betsey Chessen
1, 2, 3 to the Zoo, by Eric Carle
Roll Over! by Merle Peek
Ten Black Dots, by Donald Crews
Ten, Nine, Eight, by Molly Bang

Predictable Leveled Series

Newbridge Science—Emergent Readers, by Newbridge Educational
Scholastic Science—Emergent Readers, by Scholastic
Scholastic Social Studies—Emergent Readers, by Scholastic
The Story Box, by the Wright Group
Sunshine Nonfiction, by the Wright Group

Rhyme

I classify these books according to predominant text features.

Clap Your Hands, by Lorinda Bryan Cauley
Each Peach Pear Plum, by Janet and Allan Ahlberg
Elephants Swim, by Linda Capus Riley
In the Small, Small Pond, by Denise Fleming
In the Tall, Tall Grass, by Denise Fleming
Jesse Bear, What Will You Wear? by Nancy White Carlstrom
My Best Shoes, by Marilee Robin Burton
Shoes, by Elizabeth Winthrop
Three Little Kittens, by Paul Galdone
Zoo-Looking, by Mem Fox

Pattern

Brown Bear, Brown Bear, by Bill Martin Jr.
Cookie's Week, by Cindy Ward

Do's and Don'ts, by Todd Parr
Five Little Monkeys Jumping on the Bed, by Eileen Christelow
Five Ugly Monsters, by Tedd Arnold
From Head to Toe, by Eric Carle
Here Are My Hands, by Bill Martin Jr. and John Archambault
Quick as a Cricket, by Audrey Wood
Things That Make You Feel Good, Things That Make You Feel Bad, by Todd Parr
Time for Bed, by Mem Fox
Too Old for Naps, by Jane Yolen
The Very Busy Spider, by Eric Carle
The Very Hungry Caterpillar, by Eric Carle

Miscellaneous Nonfiction

Animal World (*Alligators, Frogs, Bears, Kangaroos, Spiders, Butterflies*, etc.), by
    Steck-Vaughn
Baby Animals (*Kangaroos, Bears, Chimpanzees, Ducklings, Elephants, Pandas*, etc.),
    by Newbridge Educational
Eyes on Nature (*Whales and Dolphins*, etc.), by Kidsbooks
Eyewitness Juniors (*Amazing Bats*, etc.), by DK
The Fascinating World of . . . (*Bees, Ants, Spiders, Frogs and Toads, Bats, Snakes*,
    etc.), by Barron's Educational
First Discovery Books (*Monkeys and Apes, Whales*, etc.), by Scholastic
See How They Grow (*Frog*, etc.), by Dutton Children's
Zoobooks magazines

Epilogue

Weaving Together the Three Domains

I first came to appreciate the love Lynnsee felt for her sister Tracie through her shares on the oval. She talked about missing Tracie and wondered when she would see her again. Through questioning, the puzzle pieces started fitting together. Tracie was Lynnsee's older sister, who was removed from the home when Lynnsee was little because, as Lynnsee said, her "mom was hurting her."

Before she started talking about her sister, Lynnsee had seemed withdrawn and lethargic, uninterested in learning. When I began to understand the loneliness she was dealing with, I encouraged her to write about the memories and dreams she held dear to her heart. "Lynnsee, I know how much Tracie means to you. I can hear it in your words and see it in your face every time you mention her. Remember, sweetheart, authors write what they know and care about. It's really sad that you and Tracie are not living together, but that's the way it is, and lots of time there's nothing we can do about it. Sometimes it can help to talk and write about our sad feelings. When you write, it's a way of talking to Tracie, even though she's not here."

Lynnsee heard my suggestion and began writing about what she felt and why. She learned words like *sad*, *lonely*, and *miss* and included them in her writing. At first, the stories were memories about her mom, brother, sister, and herself. Then she started writing about what she wished for: to have her family reunited. One entry in her daybook pictured her sitting around a table with her mom, sister, and brother. When I conferred with Lynnsee, I asked about this picture. "Is this your family at dinner?" I asked. "I thought Tracie wasn't living at home."

Lynnsee confirmed that she wasn't, saying sadly, "Tracie is away." She recorded this sentence in her daybook, ending it with an exclamation point. "Are you *excited* that Tracie is away?" I asked. She shook her head no and, without prompting, deleted her exclamation point by putting a horizontal line through it, leaving the period behind. Her picture indicated what she wished for, but her words expressed reality. I gently asked, "How do you feel about that, sweetheart?"

Solemnly, she looked at me and responded, "I am sad."

"Let's go ahead and add that, OK?" With lips pursed, she nodded her head in agreement.

The next several entries in her daybook focused on Tracie's upcoming tenth birthday. Each drawing showed the two of them together with variations of a birthday theme—a colorful cake, candles, and balloons strewn everywhere. This event obviously had major significance for Lynnsee. All the drawings included a vibrant red heart in the center of her chest and her sister's, and exclamation points were scattered throughout the writing. I learned so much about Lynnsee's thoughts by listening to her talk and reading her writing.

Lynnsee had signed up for the workbench and had already spent two days sawing and hammering pieces of wood into a freeform sculpture. The next day during choice time, she carefully adorned her creation with bottle caps and corks. All around her, the other children were busy with their own projects: Anayansi and Fidencio were finishing illustrations for their published books of riddles. Lorraine and I were engrossed in the ending to a story she'd dedicated to her grandma. Two children were painting, while several others were using big blocks to create an extensive house without a roof. Haley was rocking with Floppy in her arms while Adol was holding a book and softly singing, "All the Pretty Little Horses."

Meanwhile, without prompting, Lynnsee picked up her wooden sculpture and took it to the painting easel, where she negotiated with the painters to share the brushes. Then she unfolded a large sheet of newspaper on the floor, placed her sculpture on top, and proceeded to paint it with brilliant colors. She was proud and focused.

Several minutes later, I saw her standing at the workbench with markers and paper in hand, writing. I approached and asked, "Lynnsee, what are you doing, sweetheart?"

"I'm writing a note."

"Honey, you don't need to stand at the workbench to write a note. That's what the writing tables are for. Come over here with Lorraine and me."

Confused, she responded, "But I'm writing a note to Tracie."

Clearly I had missed something. Looking over her shoulder, I read what she had written: "HAppY BrthDa Der Tracie I HOp TaT You Lik WIWt I MaD aT SKOOL!" (*Happy Birthday, dear Tracie. I hope that you like what I made at school!*). The note made me understand what she had been intently building for three days: a present for her sister. Because she had created this sculpture at the workbench, of course that seemed like the perfect place to write the birthday note as well.

The following morning Lynnsee walked into the classroom carrying a cardboard box. I knew at once why she'd brought it and asked, "Would you like some help wrapping your birthday gift at choice time?" She smiled and nodded yes as she placed the box on the workbench.

Later that afternoon, we lined the box with bright purple and lime green tissue, colors she had chosen for her sister. She placed her project carefully inside, folding the top pieces of tissue to conceal the sculpture. We taped the treasure shut and attached her precious, loving words to the outside. Folded inside the note was a tiny marker drawing of Tracie with the now-familiar vibrant red heart in the center of her chest.

■ What We Can Learn

Lynnsee's story demonstrates the power that's generated when the three domains come together. The motive for her project originated in the emotional domain. Through observing, listening, and asking questions, I saw the learning available to her through expressing the loss of her sister. Our talks on the oval provided a safe and predictable context of sharing, which led me to encourage her to express this loss through writing (cognitive domain). And, of course, the project literally became a whole set of new learning (creative domain) as Lynnsee devised an idea for a gift for her sister, built and painted it, and then wrapped it and wrote a note to accompany it.

On days when Lynnsee shared intimate experiences on the oval, I made it a point to confer with her during writing so she could record her thoughts. Not only did she demonstrate that what we think, we can say; what we say, we can write; and what we write, we can read, but she was also able to express detailed desires and wishes that she would someday be together with Tracie. Talking about her emotions was the first step; writing about them gave her greater clarity in understanding her feelings.

Over the next few months, Lynnsee became more alive and engaged with learning in the classroom. As she began sharing experiences involving her sister, she became invested in her talk; something inside her shifted. Then, when I encouraged Lynnsee to share not just thoughts but feelings, her confidence grew as she added rich words to her writing, expanding her emotional vocabulary.

A few weeks later, her writing table buddy, Alexxus, shared a story in the author's chair about the recent death of her grandma. As Alexxus retold a cherished memory of Grandma taking her to the park and pushing her high on the swings, she broke into tears. I held her gently as the class silently and respectfully waited for her tears to stop. Then I felt a tap on my thigh as Lynnsee whispered in my ear, "Mrs. Kempton, I told Alexxus how it feels like when someone is gone. It's like my sister, because we can't see each other. I'm sad like Alexxus."

Unbeknownst to me, Lynnsee had shared this thought with Alexxus during writing workshop as she had observed her friend recording the loss of her grandma. Lynnsee had achieved enough clarity that she was able to succinctly articulate and relate her sister's loss to the death of her friend's grandmother. I asked Lynnsee to repeat to the class what she had spoken softly in my ear. Lynnsee shared her synthesis of death in slightly different words: "Alexxus' grandma died, and I can't see my sister. They're both gone." Later she wrote these powerful thoughts in her daybook. It all comes together.

Bibliography

◼ Professional Books and Articles

Beaver, Joetta M. 2005. *DRA 2 Developmental Reading Assessment*. Parsippany, NJ: Celebration.

Bissex, Glenda. 1980. *Gnys at Wrk: A Child Learns to Write and Read*. Cambridge, MA: Harvard University Press.

Fauth, B. 1990. "Linking the Visual Arts with Drama, Movement, and Dance for the Young Child." In *Moving and Learning for the Young Child*, ed. W. J. Stinson, 159–87. Reston, VA: American Alliance for Health, Physical Education, Recreation, and Dance.

Gardner, Howard. [1983] 1993. *Frames of Mind: The Theory of Multiple Intelligences*. New York: Basic.

———. 1999. *The Disciplined Mind: Beyond Facts and Standardized Testing, K–12 Education That Every Child Deserves*. New York: Simon & Schuster.

Goleman, Daniel. 1995. *Emotional Intelligence*. New York: Bantam.

Hart, Betty, and Todd R. Risley. 2003. "The Early Catastrophe: The 30 Million Word Gap by Age 3." *American Educator* 27 (Spring). www.aft.org/pubs-report/american_educator/spring 2003/catastrophe.html (accessed March 10, 2006).

Keene, Ellin Oliver, and Susan Zimmermann. 1997. *Mosaic of Thought*. Portsmouth, NH: Heinemann.

Laflamme, John G. 1997. "The Effect of Multiple Exposure Vocabulary Method and the Target Reading/Writing Strategy on Test Scores." *Journal of Adolescent & Adult Literacy* 40 (5): 372–84.

Lusche, Pat. 2003. *No More Letter of the Week*. Peterborough, NH: Crystal Springs.

McCarrier, Andrea, Gay Su Pinnell, and Irene C. Fountas. 2000. *Interactive Writing*. Portsmouth, NH: Heinemann.

National Association for the Education of Young Children (NAEYC). 1974. *The Block Book*. Washington, DC: NAEYC.

Paynter, Diane E., Elena Bodrova, and Jane K. Doty. 2005. *For the Love of Words: Vocabulary Instruction That Works*. San Francisco: Jossey-Bass.

Pitcairn, Marilyn. 2006. "Effective Literacy Instruction Is Embedded in an Orff-Based Curriculum." *The Orff Echo* (Winter): 26–29.

Public Education and Business Coalition (PEBC). 2004. *Thinking Strategies for Learners*. Denver: PEBC.

Richardson, Jan. 2005. "Levels A–I—Behaviors, Strategies, and Skills." Accessed January 5, 2007. www.readingrecovery.org/Richardson_2005Moving%20up.pdf.

Sheehan, George. No date. "Reading and Writing: Emerson." Accessed November 17, 2006. www.georgesheehan.com/essays/essay47.html.

Sher, Gail. 1999. *One Continuous Mistake*. New York: Penguin Putnam.

Sousa, David A. 2005. *How the Brain Learns to Read*. Thousand Oaks, CA: Corwin Press.

Vygotsky, Lev S. 1978. *Mind in Society: The Development of Higher Psychological Processes*. Cambridge, MA, and London: Harvard University Press.

Womack, Sara Trotman. 2006. "Focus on Research: A Research Base for Orff Schulwerk and Literacy." *The Orff Echo* (Winter): 19–20.

▨ Other Recommended Books

Calkins, Lucy McCormick. 1983. *Lessons from a Child: On the Teaching and Learning of Writing*. Portsmouth, NH: Heinemann.

———. 1994. *The Art of Teaching Writing*. Portsmouth, NH: Heinemann.

Chomsky, C. 1971. "Write First, Read Later." *Childhood Education* 47: 296–99.

Fisher, Bobbi. 1998. *Joyful Learning in Kindergarten*. Portsmouth, NH: Heinemann.

Harvey, Stephanie, and Anne Goudvis. 2000. *Strategies That Work*. York, ME: Stenhouse.

Harwayne, Shelley. 2001. *Writing Through Childhood*. Portsmouth, NH: Heinemann.

Heard, Georgia. 1989. *For the Good of the Earth and Sun: Teaching Poetry*. Portsmouth, NH: Heinemann.

Holdaway, Don. 1979. *The Foundations of Literacy*. Gosford, NSW: Ashton Scholastic.

Johnston, Peter H. 2004. *Choice Words*. Portland, ME: Stenhouse.

Miller, Debbie. 2002. *Reading with Meaning*. Portland, ME: Stenhouse.

Owocki, Gretchen. 1999. *Literacy Through Play*. Portsmouth, NH: Heinemann.

Owocki, Gretchen, and Yetta Goodman. 2002. *Kidwatching*. Portsmouth, NH: Heinemann.

Ray, Katie Wood. 1999. *Wondrous Words*. Urbana, IL: NCTE.

Ray, Katie Wood, and Lisa B. Cleaveland. 2004. *About the Authors*. Portsmouth, NH: Heinemann.

Routman, Regie. 2000. *Kids' Poems: Teaching Kindergartners to Love Writing Poetry*. New York: Scholastic.

■ Children's Literature

Abercrombie, Barbara. 1995. *Charlie Anderson*. New York: Aladdin Paperbacks.

Ahlberg, Janet, and Allan Ahlberg. 1986. *Each Peach Pear Plum*. New York: Viking Kestrel.

Allen, Judy. 2000. *Are You a Snail?* Boston: Kingfisher.

Allen, Pamela. 1980. *Mr. Archimedes' Bath*. New York: HarperCollins.

Anno, Mitsumasa. 1974. *Anno's Alphabet*. New York: Thomas Y. Crowell.

———. 1986. *Anno's Counting Book*. New York: Harper and Row.

Aragon, Jane Chelsea. 1989. *Salt Hands*. New York: Puffin Unicorn.

Arnold, Tedd. 1995. *Five Ugly Monsters*. New York: Scholastic.

Baker, Keith. 1997. *Big Fat Hen*. San Diego: Harcourt Brace.

Bang, Molly. 1983. *Ten, Nine, Eight*. New York: Scholastic.

———. 1999. *When Sophie Gets Angry—Really, Really Angry*. New York: Blue Sky.

Base, Graeme. 1986. *Animalia*. New York: Scholastic.

Berger, Barbara. 1984. *Grandfather Twilight*. New York: Philomel.

Berger, Samantha, and Betsey Chessen. 1998. *Apples*. New York: Scholastic.

Birnbaum, A. 1981. *Green Eyes*. New York: Golden.

Bove, Linda. 1985. *Sesame Street Sign Language ABC with Linda Bove*. New York: Random House.

Boyd, Lizi. 1989. *Bailey the Big Bully*. New York: Viking Kestrel.

Brinckloe, Julie. 1985. *Fireflies!* New York: Macmillan.

Brown, Margaret Wise. 1965. *The Dead Bird*. New York: HarperCollins.

Burton, Marilee Robin. 1994. *My Best Shoes*. New York: Tambourine.

Canizares, Susan, and Betsey Chessen. 1999a. *How Many Can Play?* New York: Scholastic.

———. 1999b. *Numbers All Around*. New York: Scholastic.

Carle, Eric. 1968. *1, 2, 3 to the Zoo*. New York: Philomel.

———. 1969. *The Very Hungry Caterpillar*. New York: Penguin Putnam.

———. 1971. *Do You Want to Be My Friend?* New York: HarperCollins.

———. 1984. *The Very Busy Spider*. New York: Philomel.

———. 1993. *Today Is Monday*. New York: Philomel.

———. 1997. *From Head to Toe*. New York: HarperCollins.

Carlson, Nancy. 1997. *ABC I Like Me*. New York: Puffin.

Carlstrom, Nancy White. 1986. *Jesse Bear, What Will You Wear?* New York: Macmillan.

Cauley, Lorinda Bryan. 2001. *Clap Your Hands*. New York: Putnam Juvenile.

Chessen, Betsey, and Pamela Chanko. 1998. *Counting Penguins*. New York: Scholastic.

Christelow, Eileen. 2006. *Five Little Monkeys Jumping on the Bed*. New York: Clarion.

Condra, Estelle. 1994. *See the Ocean*. Nashville, TN: Ideals Children's.

Crews, Donald. 1986. *Ten Black Dots*. New York: Greenwillow.

———. 1992. *Shortcut*. New York: Greenwillow.

Day, Alexandra. 1997. *Good Dog, Carl*. New York: Aladdin.

Demi. 1986. *Demi's Count the Animals 1 2 3*. New York: Grosset and Dunlap.

———. 1990. *The Empty Pot*. New York: Henry Holt.

Demuth, Patricia Brennan. 1994. *Those Amazing Ants*. New York: Simon and Schuster.

dePaola, Tomie. 1973. *Nana Upstairs and Nana Downstairs*. New York: Puffin.

———. 1978. *Pancakes for Breakfast*. San Diego: Voyager.

Dr. Seuss. 1963. *Dr. Seuss's ABC*. New York: Random House.

Eastman, P. D. 1974. *The Alphabet Book*. New York: Random House.

Ehlert, Lois. 1989. *Eating the Alphabet: Fruits and Vegetables from A to Z*. New York: Harcourt.

———. 1990. *Fish Eyes: A Book You Can Count On*. New York: Harcourt Brace Jovanovich.

Feelings, Muriel. 1971a. *Moja Means One*. New York: Dial.

———. 1971b. *Swahili Counting Book*. New York: Dial Books for Young People.

Fleming, Denise. 1991. *In the Tall, Tall Grass*. New York: Scholastic.

———. 1993. *In the Small, Small Pond*. New York: Scholastic.

Fox, Mem. 1988. *Koala Lou*. New York: Harcourt Brace.

———. 1993. *Time for Bed*. New York: Harcourt Brace.

———. 1996. *Zoo-Looking*. New York: Scholastic.

Galdone, Paul. 1985. *Cat Goes Fiddle-I-Fee*. New York: Clarion.

———. 1986a. *Over in the Meadow*. New York: Scholastic.

———. 1986b. *Three Little Kittens*. New York: Clarion.

Gardner, Beau. 1986. *Have You Ever Seen . . . ? An ABC Book*. New York: Dodd, Mead.

———. 1987. *Can You Imagine . . . ? A Counting Book*. New York: Dodd, Mead.

George, Lindsay Barrett. 1996. *Around the Pond: Who's Been Here*. New York: Scholastic.

Gomi, Taro. 1990. *My Friends*. Tokyo: Ehonkan.

Gray, Libba Moore. 1993. *Dear Willie Rudd*. New York: Simon and Schuster.

Grindley, Sally. 1996. *Why Is the Sky Blue?* New York: Simon and Schuster.

Grover, Max. 1993. *The Accidental Zucchini*. New York: Harcourt Brace.

Hague, Michael. 1993. *Teddy Bear, Teddy Bear Illustrated*. New York: Morrow.

Halpern, Shari. 1997. *Hush Little Baby Illustrated*. New York: North-South.

Havill, Juanita. 1989. *Jamaica Tag Along*. New York: Scholastic.

Hoban, Tana. 1983. *I Read Symbols*. New York: Greenwillow.

———. 1985. *A Children's Zoo*. New York: Greenwillow.

———. 1987. *26 Letters and 99 Cents*. New York: Greenwillow.

———. 1988. *Look! Look! Look!* New York: Greenwillow.

———. 1989. *Of Colors and Things*. New York: Greenwillow.

———. 1990. *Exactly the Opposite*. New York: HarperCollins.

Honda, Tetsuya. 1991. *Wild Horse Winter*. San Francisco: Chronicle.

Hughes, Monica. 2004. *Snails*. Creepy Creatures series. Chicago: Raintree.

Kasza, Keiko. 1992. *A Mother for Choco*. New York: Putnam and Grosset.

Keats, Ezra Jack. 1962. *The Snowy Day*. New York: Puffin.

———. 1967. *Peter's Chair*. New York: Harper and Row.

———. 1969. *Goggles!* New York: Scholastic.

Langstaff, John. 1991. *Oh, A-Hunting We Will Go*. New York: Aladdin Paperbacks.

Lionni, Leo. 1959. *Little Blue and Little Yellow*. New York: Mulberry Paperback.

———. 1963. *Swimmy*. New York: Pantheon.

Lobel, Arnold. 1981. *On Market Street*. New York: Mulberry.

London, Jonathan. 1997. *Puddles*. New York: Scholastic.

MacDonald, Suse. 1986. *Alphabatics*. New York: Trumpet Club.

Magnus, Erica. 1994. *My Secret Place*. New York: Lothrop, Lee and Shepard.

Martin, Bill Jr. 1970. *Brown Bear, Brown Bear, What Do You See?* New York: Holt, Rinehart and Winston.

———. 1991. *Polar Bear, Polar Bear, What Do You Hear?* New York: Henry Holt.

Martin, Bill Jr., and John Archambault. 1989. *Here Are My Hands*. New York: Henry Holt.

———. 2000. *Chicka Chicka Boom Boom*. New York: Aladdin Paperbacks.

Mayer, Mercer. 1968. *There's a Nightmare in My Closet*. New York: Dial.

———. 2003. *A Boy, a Dog, and a Frog*. New York: Dial.

McMillan, Bruce. 1986. *Counting Wildflowers*. New York: Lothrop, Lee and Shepard.

———. 1995. *Grandfather's Trolley*. Cambridge, MA: Candlewick.

Melloine, Bryan, and Robert Ingpen. 1983. *Lifetimes*: *The Beautiful Way to Explain Death to Children*. Toronto: Bantam.

Melmed, Laura Kraus. 1993. *I Love You as Much*. New York: Lothrop, Lee and Shepard.

Mullins, Patricia. 1993. *V Is for Vanishing: An Alphabet of Endangered Animals*. New York: Harper-Collins.

Muth, Jon J. 2002. *The Three Questions*. New York: Scholastic.

Onyefulu, Ifeoma. 1993. *A Is for Africa*. New York: Puffin.

Parr, Todd. 1999a. *Do's and Don'ts*. New York: Little, Brown.

———. 1999b. *Things That Make You Feel Good, Things That Make You Feel Bad*. New York: Little, Brown.

———. 2001. *It's Okay to Be Different*. New York: Little, Brown.

Peek, Merle. 1981. *Roll Over! A Counting Song*. New York: Clarion.

———. 1998. *Mary Wore Her Red Dress and Henry Wore His Green Sneakers*. New York: Clarion.

Penn, Audrey. 1993. *The Kissing Hand*. Washington, DC: Child Welfare League of America.

Pilkey, Dav. 1996. *The Paperboy*. New York: Scholastic.

Raffi. 1976. *Spider on the Floor*. New York: Crown.

———. 1987. *Everything Grows*. Cambridge, MA: Rounder.

———. 1988a. *Down by the Bay*. New York: Crown.

———. 1988b. *Wheels on the Bus*. New York: Crown.

———. 1989. *Five Little Ducks*. New York: Crown.

Rankin, Laura. 1991. *The Handmade Alphabet*. New York: Scholastic.

Rappaport, Doreen. 2001. *Martin's Big Words*. New York: Hyperion Books for Children.

Rathmann, Peggy. 1994. *Good Night, Gorilla*. New York: G. P. Putnam's Sons.

Riley, Linda Capus. 1995. *Elephants Swim*. New York: Houghton Mifflin.

Ryder, Joanne. 1982. *The Snail's Spell*. New York: Viking.

———. 1994. *My Father's Hands*. New York: William Morrow.

Rylant, Cynthia. 1986. *Night in the Country*. New York: Bradbury.

Saksie, Judy. 1994. *The Seed Song*. Cypress, CA: Creative Teaching.

Sandvd, Kjell B. 1996. *The Butterfly Alphabet*. New York: Scholastic.

Saport, Linda. 1999. *All the Pretty Little Horses*. New York: Clarion.

Scelsa, Greg. 1994. *Down on the Farm*. Cypress, CA: Creative Teaching.

Shore, Diane Z., and Jessica Alexander. 2006. *This Is the Dream*. New York: HarperCollins.

Shulevitz, Uri. 1974. *Dawn*. New York: Farrar, Straus and Giroux.

Sloat, Teri. 1991. *From One to One Hundred*. New York: Puffin.

Tafuri, Nancy. 1983. *Early Morning in the Barn*. New York: Greenwillow.

Thomas, Frances. 1994. *The Bear and Mr. Bear*. New York: Dutton Children's.

Van Allsburg, Chris. 1987. *The Z Was Zapped*. Boston: Houghton Mifflin.

Ward, Cindy. 1988. *Cookie's Week*. New York: Putnam.

Westcott, Nadine Bernard. 1988. *The Lady with the Alligator Purse*. New York: Little, Brown.

———. 1992. *Peanut Butter and Jelly*. New York: E. P. Dutton.

———. 2003. *Miss Mary Mack*. New York: Little, Brown.

Whippo, Walt. 2000. *Little White Duck*. New York: Little, Brown.

Wild, Margaret. 1993. *Our Granny*. Boston: Houghton Mifflin.

Wildsmith, Brian. 1983. *The Apple Bird*. Oxford: Oxford University Press.

———. 1984. *The Trunk*. Oxford: Oxford University Press.

———. 1987. *The Nest*. Oxford: Oxford University Press.

Wilhelm, Hans. 2004. *Bingo*. New York: Scholastic.

Williams, Rozanne Lanczak. 1994a. *The Bear Went Over the Mountain*. Cypress, CA: Creative Teaching.

———. 1994b. *The Bugs Go Marching*. Cypress, CA: Creative Teaching.

———. 1994c. *Cinderella Dressed in Yellow*. Cypress, CA: Creative Teaching.

———. 1994d. *Round and Round the Seasons Go*. Cypress, CA: Creative Teaching.

———. 1994e. *Way Down South*. Cypress, CA: Creative Teaching.

———. 1995a. *The Skip Count Song*. Cypress, CA: Creative Teaching.

———. 1995b. *Ten Monsters in a Bed*. Cypress, CA: Creative Teaching.

———. 1995c. *Who Took the Cookies from the Cookie Jar?* Cypress, CA: Creative Teaching.

Williams, Sue. 1989. *I Went Walking*. New York: Harcourt.

Winthrop, Elizabeth. 1986. *Shoes*. New York: HarperCollins.

Wood, Audrey. 1982. *Quick as a Cricket*. New York: Child's Play.

Woodson, Jacqueline. 2001. *The Other Side*. New York: G. P. Putnam's Sons.

Wyeth, Sharon Dennis. 1998. *Something Beautiful*. New York: Dragonfly.

Yolen, Jane. 1993. *Too Old for Naps*. New York: Harcourt Brace Jovanovich.

Young, Ed. 1989. *Lon Po Po*. New York: Philomel.

Zolotow, Charlotte. 1992. *This Quiet Lady*. New York: Greenwillow.

■ Miscellaneous Children's Nonfiction

Animal World (*Alligators, Frogs, Bears, Kangaroos, Spiders, Butterflies*, etc.). Austin, TX: Steck-Vaughn.

Baby Animals (*Kangaroos, Bears, Chimpanzees, Ducklings, Elephants, Pandas*, etc.). New York: Newbridge Educational.

Eyes on Nature (*Whales and Dolphins* etc.). Chicago: Kidsbooks.

Eyewitness Juniors (*Amazing Bats* etc.). New York: DK.

The Fascinating World of . . . (*Bees, Ants, Spiders, Frogs and Toads, Bats, Snakes*, etc.). Hauppauge, NY: Barron's Educational.

First Discovery Books (*Monkeys and Apes, Whales*, etc.). New York: Scholastic.

See How They Grow (*Frog* etc.). New York: Dutton Children's.

Zoobooks magazine. Poway: Wildlife Education.

■ Predictable Leveled Series

Newbridge Science—Emergent Readers. New York: Newbridge Educational.

Scholastic Science—Emergent Readers. New York: Scholastic.

Scholastic Social Studies—Emergent Readers. New York: Scholastic.

The Story Box. Bothwell, WA: Wright.

Sunshine Nonfiction. Bothwell, WA: Wright.

Index